Jorge Ramos

STRANGER

Jorge Ramos is an Emmy Award–winning journalist and syndicated columnist. Hailed by *Time* magazine as one of "the 25 most influential Hispanics in the United States," Ramos is the host of *America with Jorge Ramos*, a weekly show, and *Al Punto*, a Sunday-morning public-affairs show, both on Fusion.

Among his many recognitions, he received the Gabriel García Márquez Journalism Award in 2017 for excellence in journalism from the Knight Center for Journalism at the University of Texas at Austin. Ramos was also a Columbia University School of Journalism Maria Moors Cabot Prize winner in 2001 and has won eight Emmy Awards for his work as a journalist. He was honored in 2002 with the Ruben Salazar Award for Communications by UnidosUS (formerly the National Council of La Raza) for his positive portrayal of Latinos. In 2008, the Commonwealth Club of California recognized him with the Distinguished Citizen Award for being one of the outstanding individuals who embody the American Dream as an immigrant to the United States.

He writes a weekly column for more than forty newspapers in the United States and Latin America and provides three daily radio commentaries for the Univision Radio network.

Born in Mexico City, Ramos is an immigrant. He came to

the United States as a student in 1983. In November 1986, at age twenty-eight, he became one of the youngest national news anchors in the history of American television. Since then, he has been called "the voice of the voiceless" for other immigrants like him.

STRANGER

STRANGER

THE CHALLENGE
OF A LATINO IMMIGRANT
IN THE TRUMP ERA

Jorge Ramos

TRANSLATED FROM THE SPANISH BY
Ezra E. Fitz

VINTAGE BOOKS

A Division of Penguin Random House LLC

New York

A VINTAGE BOOKS ORIGINAL, FEBRUARY 2018

English translation copyright © 2018 by Ezra E. Fitz

All rights reserved. Published in the United States by Vintage Books,
a division of Penguin Random House LLC, New York, and distributed
in Canada by Random House of Canada, a division of Penguin Random
House Canada Limited, Toronto. Simultaneously published in Spanish by
Vintage Español, a division of Penguin Random House LLC, New York.
Copyright © 2018 by Jorge Ramos.

The Cataloging-in-Publication Data is on file at the Library of Congress.

Vintage Books Trade Paperback ISBN: 978-0-525-56379-2
eBook ISBN: 978-0-525-56380-8

Book design by Christopher M. Zucker

www.vintagebooks.com

Printed in the United States of America
10   9   8   7   6   5   4   3   2   1

For the Dreamers, my heroes

I have been a stranger here in my own land.
—SOPHOCLES, Antigone

*Wherever you have friends, that is your country, and
wherever you receive love, that is your home.*
—TIBETAN PROVERB

*Once there was a way
To get back homeward.*
—THE BEATLES, *"Golden Slumbers"*

Contents

STRANGER

Prologue

———

There are times when I feel like a stranger in this country where I've spent more than half my life. I'm not complaining, and it's not for lack of opportunity. But it is something of a disappointment. I never would have imagined that after having spent thirty-five years in the United States, I would still be a stranger to so many. But that's how it is.

Despite this feeling, I want to begin with gratitude. The United States is the birthplace of my children, whom I love more than anything in this world. It is here that I was able to pursue my passion and my profession—journalism—with absolute freedom. Here we can feel the energy of change: a desire for openings and innovations that can be hard to find in other parts of the world. Almost all of us here are either immigrants or the descendants of foreigners, and that has always helped us to cross borders and exceed the limits of what we thought was possible. Democracy is still the accepted political system here, and the notion of equality was established from the very moment this nation declared its independence. Here, people can live well and enjoy justice, which, in its original sense, means giving everyone his or her due.

That's why I live here. I have the wonderful circumstance and privilege—one shared by millions of people—of living in a country that accepts you with open arms. I became an American of my own free will, and the United States willingly accepted me.

Of course, none of this erases where I came from. I was born and raised in Mexico, and I will never cease to be Mexican. I love the solidarity of the Mexican people; it is a wonderful nation, one in which you will never feel alone, with a magical and incomparable history. It is an extraordinary country bursting with hopes and desires and extending its culture across the globe: a very different place from the one we see in the news, portrayed through images of violence and corrupt politicians. Most of my family still lives in Mexico. I visit them several times a year, and I am always concerned about what is happening on both sides of the border.

Both my private and public lives are binational and transnational. I am at once Mexican, American, Latino, foreigner, immigrant, emigrant, and *chilango*, among many other things. In other words, to many people, I represent the Other.

But the United States as a country has historically been accustomed to others—newcomers, those born elsewhere, those who see and speak differently—and therefore has developed a healthy tolerance for those who appear different.

But not everywhere. And not all the time.

The history of this nation registers cycles of acceptance when it comes to foreigners, followed by cycles of tremendous rejection and discrimination. This latter cycle is the one in which we are living now.

There are parts of the country that are more resistant to immigrants, blaming them unfairly for the primary problems we face, from a lack of well-paying jobs to crime. And there are politicians who take advantage of this fact in order to divide the nation and win votes. Politicians such as Donald Trump.

But let me clarify something.

This is not a book about Donald Trump. But his entry into politics and his rise to power are directly related to the growing anti-immigrant sentiment thriving across the United States. It's as bad as I've ever seen it since I first arrived here in 1983. It's as if Trump has given people permission to attack immigrants and make racist remarks, just as he has done.

Words matter. And the problem isn't limited to Trump: there are the sixty-three million Americans who voted for him and who, in many ways, think as he does. Yes, hatred has been brewing since Donald Trump stepped into the world of politics, but we cannot accept or normalize it.

Trump's attacks on immigrants and his apparent attempt to halt the demographic change that the United States is experiencing are going to fail. He is swimming against the current. He announced his campaign on June 16, 2015, but the U.S. Census Bureau subsequently published a population report estimating that as of July 1, 2015—just fifteen days later—more than half (50.2 percent) of all infants under the age of one had been born to minority parents.

The United States has never been a pure country. Conquistadores such as Juan Ponce de León and Hernando de Soto spoke Spanish in what is now the Southeast some two centuries before the first Pilgrims arrived in New England. There is evidence of the presence of Africans in our lands since the early seventeenth century. And the Native Americans preceded them all.

The very essence of the United States is to be a multiethnic, multiracial, multicultural nation, a diverse and tolerant one created by immigrants under the guiding principles of freedom, equality, and democracy.

Trump does not seem to understand this nation's history. Ultimately, we will look back on his presidency as one of the saddest moments in an already long list of racial and ethnic strife. It's as if we haven't learned anything from our past. For now, though, we will have to endure and resist it.

Sometimes, I think I've been preparing myself for this moment all my life. This is a book about what it means to be a Latino immigrant in the time of Trump. But it begins at the precise moment when one of his bodyguards threw me out of a press conference. That changed so many things for me. So this is a book about what it means to be a stranger in the United States during the first half of the twenty-first century.

"Stranger" is a word that simultaneously denotes both the foreign, *extraño*, and the foreigner, *extranjero*. That's why we decided to use it as the title for both the English and the Spanish versions of this book. It is a more complete and more inclusive title, but also a more contradictory one. How can someone who has spent more than half his life in a certain country be a stranger?

Originally, this book was going to be titled *Far from Home.* I have moved dozens of times here in the United States, and I always feel as if I'm looking for that same sense of happiness, security, and tranquility that I felt in the house where I lived for almost two decades in Mexico City.

It is, I know, an impossible search. Memories are tied not only to physical places but also to specific moments. That is why we can't return home, at least not to the house that all immigrants have left behind and that now exists only in our minds and in our memories.

This book is an explanation of my life in Mexico and the United States. But it is also an honest and sometimes painful account of what it means to live far from Mexico and, also, far from the United States. In these pages I will seek to explain this distance that I have been feeling lately in this nation where I live. This book is the work of an immigrant, and his narrative will come and go, crossing borders, without permits or papers.

Get Out of My Country

—————

G et out of my country."

I can still hear that sentence with absolute clarity, as if it occupies a specific place in my mind.

It's a scar.

Deep within.

It happened some time ago, yet it still rings in my ears as if it were yesterday. I don't even know the name of the man who said it to me. But I have his face and his hatred etched in my eyes and all over my skin.

When somebody hates you, you feel it across your entire body. It's usually just words. But the shrillness of words laden with hatred works its way under your fingernails, into your hair, around your eyelids. Of course, it also enters through your ears. Eventually, everything seems to be well-ing up somewhere between the throat and the stomach, to the point where you feel as if you're drowning. If the feeling builds up over a long enough period of time, something could burst.

The man who said "Get out of my country" was a Trump supporter. I know this because he was wearing a pin identifying the then candidate on one of his lapels. But most of all, I know this because of the way he said it to me. He looked me straight in the eyes, pointed a finger at me, and shouted.

Time and again I've gone back to watch video of the incident, which took place in August 2015, and I still don't know how I was able to remain calm. I remember the tone of his voice caught me by surprise. Trump, with the brutal and cowardly help of a bodyguard, had just ejected me from a press conference in Dubuque, Iowa. I had just started thinking about how to respond when suddenly I heard a madman shouting and pointing his finger.

I looked up, and—instead of simply ignoring his rudeness, as I would have preferred—I settled myself and simply replied, "I'm also a U.S. citizen."

His response made me laugh. "Whatever," he said, sounding like a teenager. A police officer who overheard the exchange outside the press conference stepped between us, and that was where it ended. But the hatred stuck.

Hatred is contagious.

And Trump is infectious.

I am convinced that if Trump had treated me differently, his supporter would not have spoken to me as he had. But Trump had just thrown me out of a press conference, and that, somehow, had given this man permission to direct his hatred toward me.

In over three decades as a journalist, such a thing has happened to me only once before. It was 1991, during the first Ibero-American Summit, in Guadalajara, Mexico. One of Fidel Castro's bodyguards shoved me and threw me aside as I was questioning the Cuban dictator about the lack of basic freedoms on the island.

Trump also used a bodyguard to prevent me from asking a question. He and Fidel used the same tactics of physical force—via their bodyguards—to handle an uncomfortable encounter with the press.

My problems with Trump began in New York on June 16, 2015, the day he launched his presidential campaign. It was there that he made the following statement: "When Mexico sends its people, they're not sending their best. . . . They're sending people that have lots of problems, and they're bringing those problems with us. They're bringing drugs. They're bringing crime. They're rapists. And some, I assume, are good people. . . . It's coming from more than Mexico. It's coming from all over South and Latin America. . . ."

These are racist comments. Period.

He lumped all Mexican and Latin American immigrants in the same bag. He made a sweeping generalization. He lacked the intellectual honesty to say that only some immigrants commit crimes, not the majority of them. Later, several of Trump's supporters swore that he was referring only to a specific type of undocumented immigrant—the most violent ones—not all who come across the southern border.

Perhaps. We will never know for sure. But regardless, that is not what he said. What I do know is that when Trump launched his campaign, he accused all Mexican immigrants of being criminals, drug traffickers, and rapists.

What he said is absolutely false.

All the studies I have read—especially the one conducted by the American Immigration Council—have come to the same conclusion: namely, that "immigrants are less likely to commit serious crimes or be behind bars than the native-born, and high rates of immigration are associated with lower rates of violent crime and property crime."

Trump started his path to the White House with a massive lie.

His first statements as a candidate took me by surprise. They bothered me deeply. For days and even weeks later, I felt very unsettled. I wasn't sure how to respond. As a reporter, as a Latino, and as an immigrant, I had to do something. I just didn't know exactly what. It would have to be a well-calibrated answer, not the diplomatic and aseptic response of a politician. Nor could it be an insulting jab.

Univision, the company I've been working for since January 1984, had made the courageous decision to break off its business relationship with Trump and not broadcast the Miss USA beauty pageant—which was owned in part by the businessman—on Spanish-language television for "insulting remarks about Mexican immigrants." This would mark the beginning of a lengthy legal battle.

Despite all that, I felt Trump had to be confronted on a journalistic level as well. This was not simply a business matter. So on the same day that Univision announced the end of its working relationship with Trump, I sent him a handwritten letter requesting an interview. That letter, dated June 25, 2015, read as follows:

Mr. Trump:

I want to write you personally to request an interview. But so far your team has declined.

I am sure you have a lot of things to say . . . and I have a lot of things to ask. I'll go to New York or wherever you would like.

If you would like to talk first over the phone, my personal cell is 305-794-1212.

I know this is an important issue for you as it is for me.

All the best,
Jorge Ramos

I sealed it inside a FedEx Express envelope and sent it to his New York offices. The next day, out of nowhere, I began receiving hundreds of calls and text messages, some more insulting than others. I didn't understand what was happening until a coworker of mine came into my office and said, "Trump just posted your cell phone number online."

These were some of the hundreds of texts I received:

> Jorge Ramos- Donald Trump placed your personal letter online and has your number written on it. I'm sorry about what he did.

> Go F yourself George Porgie!

> Please take the anti-U.S. Univision back to the corrupt 3rd world country Mexico and you can go with it. Thx and have a great trip back.

#Trump2016. Build those walls to stop illegals from crossing our borders.

You're a racist dirtbag. Nobody wants your illegal cousins in this country.

Trump was right ... Latinos need to stay off the 'I'm offended' bandwaggon. It's embarrasing. ... You don't speak for all Latinos!

Trump 2016! Come to this country legally or leave! Illegal is illegal!!!!

Fuck you

In fact, Trump had answered me via Instagram. He wrote, "@Univision said they don't like Trump yet Jorge Ramos and their other anchors are begging me for interviews."

Along with that brief message, he included a photograph of the letter I had written to him, without having redacted my phone number.

In addition to these messages loaded with hatred and rage, I received a lot of support. There were others, too, looking to take advantage of the situation and ask me for a job, offer me advice ... even people looking for help publishing books or recording songs.

It was clear Trump did not want to grant me an interview. However, there were other ways to confront him. Trump had just launched his presidential campaign, and one of its benefits was that he would constantly be talking to the press. That was our opportunity.

We spent nearly two months thinking about what to do. Then, one fine day, Dax Tejera—executive producer of *America with Jorge Ramos*, the program I hosted for the Fusion television network—had a great idea.

"You're not going to like what I'm about to say, but we have to go to Iowa," he said as he walked into my office and plopped down on the only sofa I have. There were many important matters to discuss, but he just sat there, waiting for my reaction.

"Iowa?" I asked. "Why do we have to go to Iowa?"

As always, Dax had done his homework. He had studied all the press conferences Trump had scheduled for the coming weeks, and the one in Iowa represented the best opportunity to meet him face-to-face. Appearances in places such as New York City would be packed with reporters, but not many news organizations would be sending their teams to cover an event in Dubuque, Iowa. Once again, Dax was right.

We contacted Trump's campaign, presented our credentials to attend the press conference in Dubuque on August 26, 2015, and though we feared the worst, nobody prohibited us from attending.

Around that same time we received a call from William Finnegan, a correspondent for *The New Yorker*, who wanted to do an article about my exchange with Trump. I invited him to join us in Iowa, and he immediately agreed. I didn't know what was going to happen there, but my intent was not to leave without confronting Trump one way or another.

I was well equipped with questions.

Trump's immigration policy would result in one of the largest mass deportations in modern history. How was he planning on deporting eleven million undocumented immigrants?

If he could amend the Constitution to strip citizenship from the children of undocumented parents, where would he be sending infants and children who had neither a country nor a passport?

Why build the largest wall on earth between two countries—1,954 miles long—if more than 40 percent of undocumented people either come by plane or overstay their visas? Wouldn't this be a monumental waste of time, money, and effort?

With these questions in hand, I left for Iowa. We arrived on-site about two hours before the press conference was scheduled to begin. We registered and set up two cameras; I sat at one end of the front row so that nothing would obstruct our view of one another, and I was wired with a microphone so that the exchange would be clearly recorded. Technically speaking, we were ready.

Television doesn't just happen. You have to create it.

But it was also important to have a plan for Trump. The first thing I decided was that I would ask my questions while standing, not seated. Body language would be vital here. I didn't want Trump to have any advantages over me. It had to be an equal exchange between the two of us. If I stood up to ask my questions, it would be that much harder for him to ignore me.

We also knew of Trump's tendency to interrupt reporters before they finish asking their questions. So I decided that I would just keep talking, refusing to be cut off, until I was through. At least with the first one.

I was ready. I had my microphone in hand and a plan to face Trump.

All of a sudden, a door opened in the back of the conference room and the security team entered, followed by Trump himself. The place fell into an unusual state of silence. The candidate greeted everyone rather unenthusiastically, barely audible, even, and then scanned the room with his eyes, as if he were taking an X-ray.

I know that kind of person. Street-smart, as you say in English. After years of interacting with people at public events, they have developed a special intuition they can use to detect both threats and opportunities. In a matter of seconds, Trump was able to identify the cameras and the reporters who were there to cover him.

He walked slowly, took his place behind the podium, gave a terse, formulaic speech, and pointed at a Fox News reporter to ask the first question. There was a single person in charge of this situation, and that person was Donald Trump.

The reporter, having been identified, asked his question. The candidate responded. And there, in that rhythm that seeks to establish itself from the outset, I detected a pause, however brief. Trump's last words were hanging in the air, and none of the other reporters were willing to jump across that void. Trump could give someone permission to speak, and he could take it away. I suppose it was something of a rite that had been established between the candidate and the elite group that had been covering his campaign for a little over two months now. Nobody wanted to shake up the rules of the game that benefited both candidate and journalists alike.

But I was new to this group. I wasn't privy to their rhythms and rituals. Plus, I had participated in hundreds of press conferences throughout my career, and I knew that you don't always have to wait for someone else to cede the floor to you. It's important to understand the pauses that inevitably arise in any exchange between people and strike quickly.

Of course, my intention coming in was to confront Trump, and it would be too risky to wait until the end of the press conference to ask my questions. We didn't know how much time Trump would give us, but it was clear that there were thousands of people waiting to see him at a campaign rally. So when I saw my opportunity, I took it.

I raised my hand, stood up from my seat, and said I had a question about immigration. I was expecting some sort of reaction, but at first nobody said anything. Not even the candidate. It was as if everyone in the room had been caught off guard. The strategy, I thought, was working, and I went ahead with my question.

But I didn't simply want to ask a question. I wanted to let Trump know that many Latinos and other immigrants were offended by his racist comments and that his own immigration proposals were based on falsehoods. After all, that's why we had gone all the way to Iowa.

But Trump is an old dog. He noticed two of the first words out of my mouth were "empty promises," and not much good was going to come after that. So without recognizing me or even looking in my direction, he scanned the hundreds of journalists in front of him, looking for someone to call on. To Trump, I didn't even exist.

In Spanish, we have a word that perfectly describes this attitude of contempt: *ningunear*. The people in power scorn, snub, or completely disregard the others. The intention is to literally turn someone into no one. And that's what Trump was trying to do with me. He didn't want to hear me or even see me.

He could have let me ask my question and given a quick, terse answer, thus disarming me. But his pride prevented him from doing that. He wouldn't be satisfied with simply denying me the opportunity to ask a question: he wanted to humiliate me, to make me an example to other reporters going forward.

But I was mentally prepared for Trump. I ignored him and continued to ask my lengthy question. I admit, it wasn't a short, simple one. I wanted to get his lies on the record first and then proceed with the questions.

Visibly upset, Trump then made a mistake. He simply couldn't allow a reporter to challenge him instead of following orders. It was then that he decided to resort to the use of force.

What follows is my first exchange with Trump:

"Mr. Trump, I have a question about immigration."

"Okay, who is next? . . . Yes, please, please." Trump was avoiding making eye contact with me while he looked for someone else to call on.

"Your immigration plan is full of empty promises."

"Excuse me. Sit down! You weren't called. Sit down! Sit down!" The strategy of standing up to ask the question seemed to be working. He wanted me to take a seat, but I was not about to do so.

"No, I'm a reporter."

"Sit down!"

"And as an immigrant and a U.S. citizen I have the right to ask a question. And the question is this."

"No, you don't. You haven't been called." At least Trump was listening to me now, I thought, so I continued to press ahead.

"No. I have the right to ask a question . . ."

"Go back to Univision."

"No, this is the question . . ."

"Go ahead," Trump said, addressing the reporter from CBS News instead of me.

"You cannot deport eleven million people. You cannot build a nineteen-hundred-mile wall. You cannot deny citizenship to children in this country . . ."

"Sit down!"

"And with those ideas . . ."

"You weren't called."

"I'm a reporter . . ." I countered.

Trump, first with a strange movement of his mouth, followed by one with his arms, called in one of his bodyguards. The man strode across the room, stopped in front of me, and grabbed me by my left forearm before dragging me out of the room.

"Don't touch me, sir," I said.

The security officer said I was being "disruptive" and that I should wait my turn to ask a question. But I insisted that as a reporter, I had the right to do so. He asked to see my credentials, and I said that they were with my briefcase next to my seat. I also kept telling him not to touch me, but he didn't care. He kept on shoving me and didn't release my forearm until we were out of the room.

Just then, one of Trump's supporters—campaign button and all—followed me out of the conference room and confronted me.

"You are very rude. It's not about you," he said, jabbing his finger at me.

"It's not about you, either," I said. My mind was still on the incident with Trump and his security guard. There were many things I could have said, but there, in the moment, I decided not to focus my indignation at this supporter. He, however, was insistent:

"Get out of my country. Get out! This is not about you."

"I'm also a U.S. citizen."

"Well, whatever. No. Univision, no. It's not about you."

"It's not about you. It's about the United States."

A police officer who overheard our conversation stepped in between us. And that was the end of our exchange of words.

My producer, Dax Tejera, and I had to decide what to do next. Trump would have to walk out the same door I exited, and one of my cameramen was ready in case I wanted to approach the candidate a second time.

I decided not to leave. I had gone to Iowa to talk to Trump, and I would try again outside the conference room.

After I was forcibly expelled, two other reporters—Kasie Hunt of MSNBC and Tom Llamas of ABC News—came to my defense and challenged Trump hard. Why did he have me kicked out of the press conference?

"I don't know really much about him," he told them. "I don't believe I've ever met him, except he started screaming. I didn't escort him out. You have to talk to security; whoever security is has escorted him out. But certainly he was not chosen. I chose you, I chose other people. He just stands up and starts screaming. So, you know, maybe he's at fault also. I don't even know where he is. I don't mind if he comes back, frankly."

It was quite telling that Trump told the members of the press that he didn't know who I was. After all, he had published my letter online just two months earlier. Besides, during our exchange in the conference room, he had specifically told me to "go back to Univision." If he truly didn't know who I was, how did he know who I worked for?

The answer is that Trump was lying.

All of a sudden, his press secretary came out of the room. "Hi, I'm Hope Hicks," she said, waving to me. She asked if I would like to go back into the conference, and I said yes. But I cautioned her that my one condition was that I be allowed to ask my questions. She agreed and asked me to wait until Trump gave me the floor.

I went back into the conference room. I never found out whether it was her decision to let me back in or if she made the move only when she heard what the candidate said after I was escorted out.

I returned to my seat, which was still empty. My briefcase with my press credentials was still there as well. I raised my hand to ask a question, and—as if by following some sort of magical choreography—Trump pointed to me and said, "Yes, good, absolutely. Good to have you back."

The exchange we then had went unnoticed by most news networks. The headlines around the world would be about how I was forcibly expelled from a press conference by one of his bodyguards, not about our conversation after the fact.

Finally, I had my chance to confront Trump. What follows is the central tenet of our conversation, edited so that the exchange can be better understood:

"So here's the problem with your immigration plan. It's full of empty promises. You cannot deport eleven million undocumented immigrants. You cannot deny citizenship to the children [of undocumented parents] of this country."

"Why do you say that?"

"You have to change the Constitution, Mr. Trump."

"Well, a lot of people think that an act of Congress can do it. Now it's possibly going to have to be tested in courts. . . . [If] a woman is getting ready to have a baby, she crosses the border for one day and has the baby, all of a sudden for the next eighty years we have to take care of the people."

"The Constitution [says that]."

"No, no, no. I don't think so. I know some of the television scholars agree with you. But some of the great legal scholars agree that's not true."

"You are not answering, Mr. Trump."

"I am answering. . . . It's going to be tested, okay?"

"Anyway, the question is, how are you going to build a nineteen-hundred-mile wall?"

"Very easy. I'm a builder. That's easy. I build buildings that are ninety-four stories. Can I tell you what's more complicated? What's more complicated is building a building that's ninety-five stories tall, okay?"

"But it's an unnecessary waste of time and money."

"You think so? Really? I don't think so. . . ."

"Almost forty percent of the [undocumented] immigrants come by plane, they simply overstay their visas."

"I don't believe that. I don't believe it. . . ."

"Well, they are coming by plane."

"Well, they are coming by many different ways. But the primary way they're coming is right through, right past our border patrols."

"How are you going to deport eleven million undocumented immigrants? By bus? Are you going to bring the army?"

"Let me tell you. We're going to do it in a very humane fashion. Believe me. I've got a bigger heart than you do. . . . The one thing we are going to start with immediately are the gangs and the real bad ones. . . . We have tremendous crime, we have tremendous problems. . . . Those people are out. They're going to be out so fast your head will spin. Remember you used the word 'illegal' immigrant?"

"No, I did not use that word."

"Well, you should use the word because that's what the definition is."

"No human being is illegal."

"Okay, well, when they cross the border, from the legal standpoint, they are illegal immigrants when they don't have their papers."

"How do you deport eleven million?"

"You know what it's called? Management. See, you're not used to good management because you are always talking about government."

"Just imagine—"

"Let me just tell you. Wait, wait, wait. Government is incompetent."

"You are not giving specifics."

"I've given you specifics. I've given you specifics. Great management."

But the exchange did not end there. Other reporters asked their questions, and then I raised my hand again. Trump, apparently, was willing to continue the debate. I stood up and began, once more:

"You are not going to win the Latino vote."

"I think so, because I'm going to bring jobs back."

"The truth is—I've seen the polls—a Univision poll that says seventy-five percent of Latinos—"

Here is where he interrupted me. Instead of acknowledging that several polls indicated that he was losing the Latino vote, he brought up the lawsuit he had filed against Univision.

"How much am I suing Univision for right now? Do you know the number? Tell me."

"The question is—"

"Do you know the number? How much am I suing Univision for?"

"I'm a reporter, Mr. Trump."

"Five hundred million."

"I'm a reporter and the question is—"

"And they're very concerned about it, I have to say."

"So allow me to ask the question."

"Go ahead."

"You're losing the Latino vote."

"I don't think so."

"Seventy-five percent of Latinos have a negative opinion of you. Gallup considers you the most unpopular candidate of all [Republicans]. Just check social media."

"Do you know how many Latinos work for me? Do you know how many Hispanics are working for me?"

"Many Latinos detest you and despise you, Mr. Trump."

"They love me."

"That is not true. See the polls, Mr. Trump."

"Do you know how many Hispanics work for me? Thousands."

"Nationwide, seventy-five percent [of Latinos] have a negative opinion of you. You won't win the White House without the Latino vote."

"Here's what happens. Once I win you're going to see things happen. You know what they want? They want jobs. That's what they want."

"And they want to be treated fairly."

This conversation was going nowhere. I was citing poll numbers that showed his huge unpopularity among Latino voters, and he was insisting that Latinos loved him and that thousands work for him.

At that time, I was convinced that nobody could win the White House without a significant portion of the Latino vote. Mitt Romney earned only 27 percent of the Latino vote in 2012, paving the way for Barack Obama's reelection. And years earlier, in the 2008 presidential election, Senator John McCain also lost to Barack Obama, having garnered only 31 percent of the Hispanic vote.

Everything seemed to indicate that the Republican candidate, whoever it might be, would be barely able to reach a third of the Latino vote, which would not be enough to win the presidency. In 2016, there were 27.3 million registered Latino voters, and even though only about half of them were expected to cast ballots, their influence would be definitive. Or so I thought.

After my exchange with Trump at the press conference, the candidate wanted to continue the debate.

"You and I will talk. We're going to be talking a lot, Jorge Ramos."

"I hope that we can have that conversation."

"We will. We will."

"Okay."

We never spoke again.

The media, both in the United States and internationally, focused its attention on the fact that I was kicked out of the press conference: a direct attack on freedom of expression and an apparently unprecedented event in a U.S. presidential campaign. Everything I had asked Trump was relegated to the background. However, in his responses, we can see the foundations of the anti-immigrant proposals that he would look to implement once he set foot in the White House.

The road proposed by Trump was fraught with danger. I saw it. Many other Latino reporters saw it as well, and together we denounced it. Trump's words were a real threat to millions of immigrants. And I always took them seriously. To consider him a clown or a madman would be a grave mistake. He's neither of these things. In fact, one of the most troubling features of Trump's personality is that he almost never laughs. I haven't seen this happen once.

As reporters, we would have to be a lot tougher with him in the wake of the announcement of his campaign. His attacks on immigrants were brutal. But by the end of summer 2015, Trump had become a true media phenomenon, and the major television networks were willing to give him nearly all the time he wanted in exchange for ratings.

To be frank, Trump was almost always willing to give interviews and make public statements on multiple issues. The other Republican candidates were not nearly as accessible. And by the time they realized their mistake, it was too late.

But this policy of open access was never extended to the Spanish-language media in general or to Univision in particular. Despite the candidate's promise that we would speak again, we had, for all intents and purposes, been banned.

Despite the fact that Trump had said he would be willing to talk with me further and possibly even grant us an interview, his anti-immigrant rhetoric and agenda would no longer allow this to happen. He was operating as the enemy of the undocumented, and his confrontation with me was just one more way of advancing his message.

And what was that message? If Trump was willing to forcibly eject a legal immigrant with a U.S. passport and a nationally broadcast television show from a press conference, he would have no problem expelling the more vulnerable immigrants from the country. Granting an interview or engaging in a dialogue with a Univision journalist—or any other Spanish-language media outlet—just wasn't suited to his plan to criminalize a defenseless minority.

Trump had defended his position, and so had I.

I've been accused of being an activist. I'm not. I'm simply a journalist who asks questions.

But when there's a politician such as Donald Trump who consistently lies, who makes racist, sexist, and xenophobic comments, who attacks judges and journalists, and who behaves like a bully during a presidential campaign, you cannot remain neutral. To do so would be to normalize his behavior. And such behavior is not a good example, especially for children. Our primary social duty as journalists is to question those who have and those who seek power.

That's why I did not sit down and did not shut up at the press conference in Iowa. In one way or another, I had been preparing for that moment my entire career.

For more than three decades, I have had the opportunity to work with absolute freedom as a reporter in the United States. Censorship was why I left Mexico in the first place, and I wasn't about to shut up now.

But the nation that had offered me complete freedom of speech and the promise of equality was changing dramatically. A certain segment of American society, often outside the eyes of mainstream media, was displaying a growing anxiety and resentment against minorities and foreigners. This segment was mistakenly blaming them for their personal misfortunes and the larger problems affecting the nation.

This phenomenon was not a new one. It started gaining momentum after Barack Obama first took office, and despite the inherent sense of irrationality, it had been searching for legitimacy and representation among the more conservative groups in the country. Trump wasn't the leader of that movement, but he read it well and worked it to his electoral advantage.

This is how I gradually became a stranger in the country where I had lived for more than half my life. The land where my two children were born.

In the end, I have to admit that when I heard the cry of "Get out of my country," it took me by surprise.

In fact, it still rings in my ears to this very day.

Far from Home

———

You can't go home again," wrote the Spanish author Javier Cercas, quoting Bill Bryson. And after reading it in his book, *Agamemnon's Truth*, it made me want to scream. Don't tell me that, Javier! Please! I've spent half my life thinking about returning home!

Returning home is almost an obsession for those of us who left. Sometimes there are concrete plans, but otherwise there is simply an intense desire to recover the sense of security and happiness that we once enjoyed.

When we say "home," we're not necessarily talking about a specific place. More than anything, it has to do with the idea of belonging to something, of feeling that we come from a specific slice of the planet and that the people who continue to live there will still love and care for us.

The problem is that this "home" is an idealized one. It started changing the very moment we left. The dynamics are modified when one of the family members leaves. Further, the internal perception of what our "home" is can be tied to a specific moment. The home that I miss is where I grew up as a child and later as a teenager in the 1960s and 1970s. And while I could physically live there again, the home I long for is gone now. But still, I keep looking for it. Each and every day.

The subtitle of one of my books is *A Journalist's Search for Home.* That's what I'm talking about here: searching for my place in the world.

I have moved so many times between Miami and Los Angeles that I've forgotten the addresses. But I'll never forget the street—Hacienda de Piedras Negras—and the number of the house where I grew up in the Bosques de Echegaray neighborhood of massive Mexico City.

I left, but I didn't want to.

Immigrants don't leave home because they want to. They are almost forced to become foreigners in a new land. A very powerful force is expelling them while something equally strong is drawing them to another country. It's much more than a simple exploratory adventure. When the conditions of expulsion and attraction line up, the decision to emigrate is made.

Who would want to leave their family and friends? The idea should be to grow, work, and live alongside those who love you. But that's not always possible.

"Little is more extraordinary than the decision to migrate, little more extraordinary than the accumulation of emotions and thoughts which finally leads a family to say farewell to a community where it has lived for centuries, to abandon old ties and familiar landmarks, and to sail across dark seas to a strange land."

These words, which John F. Kennedy wrote in his book *A Nation of Immigrants*—which was published in 1958, the same year I was born—make me think that the assassinated former president understood perfectly well what it means to be an immigrant. After all, his eight great-grandparents all crossed the Atlantic after leaving Ireland for the United States.

And I agree. Becoming an immigrant was the most difficult—and the most extraordinary—decision of my life.

Along with my gratitude to the United States for having welcomed and accepted me, there is a genuine longing for what I left behind in Mexico. The geographic proximity, the shared border, shared cell phone and digital technology, and hundreds of flights have kept me in close and frequent contact with Mexico during all these years. But as much as I've made an effort to be aware of what's going on in my country of origin, distance and ignorance have been imposing themselves little by little. Reading about Mexico and seeing reports about what's going on there on television or the Internet isn't the same as living there.

Much to my regret (and sometimes painfully so), I have come to the realization that I have lost the ability to endure the spiciest of Mexican salsas. What I wouldn't even have blinked at years ago would now make me cry . . . and I say "would" because I won't even dare try them anymore. My tongue and stomach have been keeping their distance for so long that they're beginning to impose their will on me. And something similar has been happening between me and the country itself. Of course, Mexico is not the same nation it was when I left, and I have been losing touch with what the Mexican people love and with what makes them cry. I can imagine it and sometimes I can even see it, but after thirty-five years of separation, I can no longer claim to understand it all . . . regardless of what my taste buds might have to say.

Stranger

———

The English word "stranger" reflects, both accurately and painfully, the way I often feel here in the United States. A stranger is someone who doesn't belong here, who comes from somewhere else. An intruder who poses a danger to the group. But most of all, a stranger is someone unknown.

I've been working in Spanish-language television in the United States for over three decades and I am still a stranger to millions of Americans. Of course, some may have seen me on a television show in English, read one of my articles, or followed me on Twitter or Facebook. But that doesn't mean that I feel like a part of their community.

I will always be a stranger.

I am the Other.

I am the outsider.

I am a stranger.

Despite the fact that my two children were born in the United States. Despite the fact that I have become an American citizen and carry a blue passport. Despite having lived here since 1983. Despite having done everything that has to be done in order to integrate: learn English, pay taxes, study the customs, respect the traditions, and contribute as much as I can to the nation that adopted me.

But none of this seems to have been enough.

Maybe the problem was with my expectations. Yes, I'm an immigrant, born in Mexico. But I thought that after having spent more than half my life in the United States, I would feel totally accepted by my new country.

But that hasn't been the case.

The plan didn't quite take shape. One would think that an immigrant would be able to integrate with relative ease into a nation created by immigrants. But I never expected there would be so much resistance trying to prevent this from ever happening.

I've often thought that it might be my own fault. I have many friends and colleagues who are Americans and speak only English. But once I came to Los Angeles, I connected with people who speak Spanish—people who are foreigners like me—and perhaps it doesn't help much that I have always worked for a television network that broadcasts in Spanish for Latinos and Latin Americans. People could, to some extent, blame me for getting away from the essence of the nation— even though that essence is rapidly changing—and for choosing to live on one of the coasts: the outskirts. But to be honest, that's where I felt most comfortable.

I am one of those people who speak with an accent, who move between cultures, who jump from country to country and from language to language. One of those who come from somewhere else and have grown accustomed to being a minority. We did not inherit money, power, or influence. Everything we have came as a result of hard work. Our natural state is to move, to shift, to change.

We have undergone many transformations along the way, beginning with the way we refer to ourselves. Sometimes we are Mexicans, Guatemalans, Venezuelans, or Argentines. Other times we're Latinos or Hispanics. Maybe we're Cuban Americans or some other compound nationality that ends with "American." Perhaps we're just Americans. Often it's all of the above or a curious combination of terms: my son, Nicolás, for example, considers himself Ricancubanmexicanamerican, and my daughter, Paola, is Cuban, Spanish, Mexican, and American and could have up to three passports.

But commingling seems to frighten some Americans. No matter how hard we try to recite the Pledge of Allegiance in perfect English or sing "The Star-Spangled Banner" with gusto, we will never be seen as truly a part of the same melting pot as them.

I am one of the Others.

Saying that the United States is our country, too, is a move that is both daring and—to some—unforgivable. Once, during the broadcast of the Lo Nuestro Awards, which honor the best of Latin music, I was invited to give a brief speech. It was less than a minute, but it was there that I said, "This is our country, not theirs."

Donald Trump had just taken office, and some of his constituents assumed that the time for retribution was near. But in spite of that, I said the United States was our country . . . because it is.

The United States is for all Americans, regardless of race, religion, or ethnic origin. It is not just for the white majority, for those who voted for Trump, or for the wealthy. It is even less so for the racists or the white supremacist groups that have been appearing with alarming frequency of late.

In many ways, the United States also belongs to the immigrants and foreigners who have contributed so much to its greatness. How could we take credit away from those who feed us, those who build our houses, those who care for our children? How could we diminish all the international students and visitors who teach in our schools and conduct research at our universities?

How could we forget all the immigrants whose investments, contributions, and inventions have placed the United States at the forefront of the scientific, artistic, financial, and medical fields? According to a report published in 2011 by the Partnership for a New American Economy, over 40 percent of the 2010 Fortune 500 company founders were either immigrants themselves or the children of immigrants. This report also states that major U.S. brands such as Apple, Google, AT&T, Colgate, eBay, General Electric, IBM, and McDonald's, among many others, were created by either immigrants or their children.

So, yes, the United States is our country.

It belongs to all of us.

Foreigners and natural-born citizens alike.

It's as much mine as it is yours.

After saying something as simple as that, I received multiple verbal attacks on social networks and from some of the more conservative members of the national media. My critics found it inconceivable that they should have to share "their country" with us. Their minds couldn't grasp the notion that others—the outsiders—could also be part and parcel of the United States.

Of course, some assumed that when I said "our country," I was referring only to Latinos and immigrants. That was not the case. Immigrants from Latin America and the rest of the world, who have spent years living here in the United States, do not want to be—nor could they ever be—the sole proprietors of this nation. But at the same time, no one can take away our right to say that this country belongs to us as much as it does to anyone.

But there is still a great deal of resistance when it comes to integrating all the varied groups that make up the United States. Just look at Twitter.

On March 12, 2017, Iowa congressman Steve King referenced Dutch right-wing politician Geert Wilders, tweeting that "Wilders understands that culture and demographics are our destiny. We can't restore our civilization with somebody else's babies."

What civilization does Congressman King and others like him want to restore? Does it include all of us or only white people of European descent?

During the 2016 presidential campaign, director Catherine Tambini, producers Verónica Bautista and Dax Tejera, and I were filming a documentary called *Hate Rising*. Our goal was to denounce the dangerous growth of racist groups and their expressions of hatred across the United States. But even more important, it was about trying to understand why those who hate us do so.

We toured the nation. I spoke with a Muslim woman who was attacked in a restaurant—her face was cut and bloodied by another customer wielding a beer mug—for talking with her relatives in a language other than English. I listened to tearful schoolchildren who were afraid their parents would be deported when Trump's new anti-immigrant policies were implemented. I stood with a homeless Mexican cancer patient who was kicked in the streets by supporters of the Republican presidential candidate. I witnessed the tragedy that afflicted the LGBTQI community in the wake of the attack on the Pulse nightclub in Orlando, Florida. I received information from the valiant and invaluable Southern Poverty Law Center on how white supremacist groups operate in the United States. And I interviewed members of the Ku Klux Klan and the so-called alt-right movement.

One of the people I interviewed told me, to my face and without the slightest hint of irony, that eventually I would be forced to leave the country simply because I am Hispanic. He said that he fought for white people the same way that I fight for Latinos. The difference—the big difference—is that I'm not trying to exclude anyone from this nation, while he is hoping to exclude me and other minorities.

But that wasn't the only sign of rejection I received.

At a remote Texas estate on private property, one of the local Klan leaders assured me that he was superior to me by the simple fact of being white. When I told him that—despite whatever else he may think—the United States is our country, both his and mine, he couldn't contain himself and spat out three words: "It is not." I did not shake his hand after the interview. It was clear to me that he didn't even want to touch me.

These are the reasons I feel like a foreigner in America.

The truth of the matter is that I will never be American enough for many Americans. Just as I will never be Mexican enough for many Mexicans.

I live the life of a stranger.

My Road North

———

My process of becoming Americanized has been a long, unpredictable, and incomplete one.

When I was a child, all I knew of the United States was the television show *Combat!* and the songs of that era, which I listened to on the radio in my dad's car.

I don't think I was even ten years old when I came here for the first time. My paternal grandparents, Gilberto and Raquel Ramos, would drive from Mexico City to Laredo, Texas, once a year to buy all the things they couldn't get in Mexico, from clothes and medicine to cooking utensils and toys for us.

Their return was always highly anticipated by the entire family. They came bearing gifts for all of us, including candy that we couldn't get in Mexico: American brands of chewing gum and chocolate, along with some sweetened lemon candies that I absolutely loved.

Once, on our way to the movies, I got one of those candies stuck in my throat, and my dad had to hang me upside down by my feet to get it out before I choked. I never ate one of them again. But I still felt lucky. The United States was a wonderful place filled with sweets that we couldn't get in Mexico.

America always fascinated me. What could such a place be like? I never could have imagined that many years later it would become my home.

One day, my grandfather told my parents that he wanted to invite me to join him on his annual trip to Laredo. I happily accepted. I remember buying several comic books to read during the daylong journey, and I slept for hours in the back of his car.

We stopped overnight with some relatives in Ramos Arizpe, in the state of Coahuila, and the next day we drove to the border. I don't remember any complications that day when we entered the United States by car. The traffic lights and the general cleanliness of Laredo were the first things that struck me . . . but more than anything, it was the stores. I went with my grandparents on all their shopping trips. And what I noticed was that there was so much of everything. Unlike Mexico, the United States was a land of abundance.

My second trip to the United States was with the entire family. After saving up for years, my dad took my siblings and me to Disneyland. It was every child's dream. The organization and refinement of the amusement park and its surroundings, with the immaculate gardens and freshly cut grass, contrasted with the chaos of the Mexico City I came from.

What I didn't know at the time was that these two trips

would leave a lasting mark on my mind and would influence the decisions I would make nearly two decades later.

I spent my teenage years in Mexico listening to more music in English than in Spanish. I still remember how the radio stations would pit Los Bítles (which is what we called the Beatles) against the Monkees and have listeners call in to support their favorite group. The soundtrack of my life was filled with songs by James Taylor, Jim Croce, Elton John, Cat Stevens, and John Denver. At parties we would dance to Chicago and Stevie Wonder, and we always waited for a slow song by the band Bread so we could dance with the girls we had crushes on. The funny thing is that most of the time my friends and I hummed along with these tunes and even sang the words phonetically, even though we had no idea what the lyrics actually meant.

My English had a distinct tinge of background music.

After finishing high school in Mexico City, two of my best friends, Benjamín Beckhart and Gloria Meckel, made plans to attend college in the United States. Benjamín went on to Wharton in Philadelphia, while Gloria chose Rice University in Houston. I was very jealous of them.

Our family didn't have the money to allow me to attend a private university in Mexico, much less in the United States. But I made my plans. I submitted applications to several schools in both the United States and the United Kingdom and applied for one of the scholarships offered by the Mexican government to study abroad. After jumping through several cumbersome bureaucratic hoops, I was denied the scholarship.

I had no choice but to stay in Mexico.

I studied for a career in communications, taking day classes at the Universidad Iberoamericana while working afternoon shifts at a travel agency to pay for school. A couple of years later, I got a job with Mexico's primary radio station, XEW, which was known as "the Voice of Latin America from Mexico." I was still studying communications, and working in radio seemed to be more in accordance with my future aspirations.

I was an assistant there. My job was to help everyone with everything. The station manager didn't think I had the kind of voice for radio, so I was limited to research and writing copy for other reporters and broadcasters.

But everything changed on March 30, 1981.

A gunman, John Hinckley, Jr., had tried to assassinate Ronald Reagan coming out of a hotel. The wounded president was being cared for at a Washington hospital, and the world was holding its breath.

When news of the attempt reached us, the director entered the newsroom, gathered all the staff together, and asked, "How many of you speak English?" A few of us raised our hands. "And how many of you have your passports and visas in order?" That left only me. "Ramos, you're going to Washington right now," he ordered.

And I was off.

I was by far the least experienced reporter in that newsroom, and I had never been sent out to cover a story anywhere. I was barely an assistant to the assistant. But the rudimentary English I learned in high school and my obsession with always having a valid passport gave me my first big opportunity.

My work, I must admit, left much to be desired. I didn't

know how to conduct a good interview or how to compose a report for radio. But I did.

Besides the enormous professional challenge, the most important thing for me was to experience a piece of history taking place in the capital of the most powerful nation on earth. Little was known at the time about Hinckley's motivations and background, and there were times when many people feared that President Reagan might not survive. The eyes of the world were on Washington, and I was there.

Before taking that trip, I had thought of becoming a psychoanalyst, a university professor, or even a politician. But after that experience, I was convinced that I wanted to dedicate my life to journalism. I wanted to be on the scene when history was being made, and I wanted to get to know the people who were making it. Plus, someone else would be paying for my plane tickets. It was a perfect combination.

Upon my return, I understood that, with very few exceptions, Mexican radio would not allow me to travel the world as a reporter. To do that, I would have to make the move to television. So I formed a plan.

I got a job as a copywriter on a television newscast at Televisa, and later I was given the opportunity to work as a correspondent on the program *60 Minutos* (named after the original show, *60 Minutes*, in the United States).

I hadn't been able to attend college in the United States, but my career was moving fast. I got to cover the eruption of the Chichonal volcano in March 1982. We got so close to the event that ash leaked into the engine of the car we were traveling in, rendering it useless, a total loss. My crew and I were stuck in a gorge where the gases were quickly building up and could potentially explode at any moment because of the intense heat. Finally, a group of local peasants who were also fleeing through the gorge helped us escape the danger.

But I was also interested in other types of eruptions.

In just my third report, I criticized the Mexican president for the lack of democracy in the country. From 1929 through 2000, Mexican presidents were chosen *por dedazo*, which means that the incumbent leader can literally point with his finger and choose his successor. It was obvious to everyone. But, surprisingly, nothing was said about this on television, which was why I thought it would make a good story. Well, not everyone thought this was the best idea.

At that time, in the early 1980s, there was a direct line of censorship extending from the president to the media. No news got reported without the blessing of the Mexican government. So my boss—who, by the way, was also the coach of a professional soccer team—ordered me to change parts of the story. When I refused, he had another reporter rewrite what I had written. I wasn't going to allow myself, as a journalist, to be censored. Working in television was the opportunity I had been looking for all my life, but I wasn't willing to do it at any cost. I thought it over for a couple of days, and finally I turned in my letter of resignation on June 28, 1982. "What I was asked to do," I wrote, "goes against my principles, my professionalism, and my sense of honesty. . . . To have done so would have contradicted the clearest, most basic idea of what journalism is: the pursuit of the truth."

And with that, I was out of television.

I remember delivering several copies of my resignation letter to the owner of the company and the board of directors. I went home, looked at my mother, and said, "I just burned the ships." I was young, but everything was crystal clear to me.

And that decision to reject censorship had an impact on the rest of my life.

I had just graduated from college, but I was out of work and out of money, and just about every door in Mexican media had been closed to me.

So, at just twenty-four years of age, I made the most difficult and significant decision of my young life. I had to give up not only Mexican television, but Mexico itself.

The conclusion was a clear one: If I had just been censored by the most important television station in Mexico, what could I expect from other, smaller venues?

I sold my *bochito*—a beat-up old Volkswagen Beetle—scratched together a few dollars, left my home, my friends, and my family, the street corners and flavors I knew and loved, and bought a one-way ticket to Los Angeles, California.

That was January 2, 1983.

People are not born with the idea of becoming an immigrant. Most of the time it happens when you are forced to leave your country. This is the same story told by the 250 million immigrants around the world.

I am one of them.

I remember well the first day I arrived in my adoptive nation. It's something an immigrant never forgets. The sun was setting and it was almost dark. But what I remember most is walking across a parking lot and realizing that everything I owned—a suitcase, a guitar, and a few documents—could be carried by my own two hands.

I never quite felt that same sense of complete and utter freedom again in all my life.

I was there on a student visa. UCLA offered a one-year extension course on television and journalism, and they had accepted me. But first I had to learn English well . . . or at least well enough to pass the course.

It wasn't easy. I had studied English in elementary school and a bit in high school, but my handling of the language was rudimentary at best. The songs I remembered in English contained lyrics that, in fact, meant nothing to me. As often happens when you are learning a new language, you understand it more than you can speak it. I struggled in my first few writing classes, but my instructors at UCLA were very understanding. I was starting practically from scratch. To this day I remember a line I used to justify my inability to communicate properly: "I'm still learning English, but I have no command of the language."

When I told my classmates that I was from Mexico, one of the most common responses was, "But you don't look Mexican." It was one of my first encounters with the rigid stereotypes that existed in the United States when it came to immigrants. Yes, I had light brown hair and greenish-blue eyes, but I was still from Mexico.

Decades later, the prejudice was still there. A television host told me he couldn't understand why I was Latino if I was whiter than him. Clearly he didn't understand that Latinos are not a different race, just a different ethnic group.

During a visit to a local station in L.A., I naively asked the news director if he thought I would ever be able to work as a reporter in the United States. His answer was brutal yet honest: he said that I'd never be able to do it with English skills as basic as mine. But then he added something that surprised me: he said that I wouldn't be able to work much in my own language, either. In his opinion, Spanish-language media would soon disappear because Latinos were rapidly assimilating.

He was right about working in English. There were times when I couldn't even understand what he was saying. It took over three decades before I got my first English-language program on the Fusion network. But that director was flat-out wrong about the future of Spanish-language television.

The early 1980s saw a rapid growth in the Hispanic population of America. As a community, we would grow from about fifteen million to fifty-five million in just over thirty years. I was, in fact, riding the crest of the Latino wave.

I managed to survive my first year as a student there on what little I had. My diet consisted of a lot of bread, lettuce, and a few little boxes of rice and noodles that we secretly warmed up in our room there at the Pink House. That's what we called the brightly colored home near UCLA that was run by a Mexican man and was used by some of the students as a residence. It wasn't entirely legal to rent rooms in the upscale Westwood neighborhood, but it was the only thing available to those of us who couldn't afford to pay for private apartments or dorm rooms on campus.

The half-dozen other students who also stayed in the house did not have access to the kitchen, so we warmed our meals on hot plates in the closets—and even the bathrooms—without the owner ever realizing it. Eating out was a luxury we simply couldn't afford.

The Pink House was my first big lesson in diversity and tolerance in the United States. I started out sharing a small room with Charles, a descendant of the Ashanti people in

Ghana, before moving into one a little bit larger (though the bed had a huge depression in the middle of it) with Emil from Iran. I had long conversations about religion with Hashmi, a Muslim student from Pakistan, and I crossed paths with students from Brazil, South Korea, and other parts of the globe.

The atmosphere at the Pink House was full of energy. There's nothing like discovering the world for the first time on a shoestring budget. Everything seems at once an adventure and a privilege. But the house was also filled with nostalgia.

Once I saw a pile of letters Charles had sent to his partner in Ghana that had been returned to him. For some reason, they were marked as being unable to deliver. Charles sobbed inconsolably for days, and I never found out if his relationship was able to endure that awful postal mishap.

I don't know how, but Jorge, the owner, was able to get a pay phone installed on the ground floor. Our families often called us there on the weekends. Back then, it was very expensive to make international phone calls. Once, one of the students managed to rig a quarter with a tiny string so it could be deposited and then pulled back up and out of the slot. Thanks to that trick, we were able to save a few dollars and still call home with no time limits . . . that is, until the phone company found out what we were doing and temporarily cut off service to that pay phone. We couldn't communicate with our families for months, which was a real blow to us all.

To better learn English and get to know the United States a little more, I bought a device that had a small black-and-white television, a radio, and a cassette player. That cheap little apparatus turned out to be a great teacher. On it I was able to watch programs in English and practice the pronunciation of a language that had, up to that point, been rebelling against me.

It was also where I saw my first Spanish-language newscast, on KMEX, Channel 34, in Los Angeles. My classes at UCLA were mostly at night, so on the days when I didn't have to go to campus, I always caught the local six o'clock news.

Before I left Mexico, a friend of mine gave me the name of the Channel 34 news director, Pete Moraga. One day I called to ask if I could meet with him, and he kindly agreed despite having no idea who I was. I was about to finish my yearlong extension course, and I would be able to work for up to two years with an adjustment to my visa known as "practical training." Besides, I didn't want to go back to Mexico empty-handed. I asked him for a job.

The first time we met he said that he didn't have anything available but that we should keep in touch, which I did. The second time, he said yes.

On January 2, 1984, exactly one year after I arrived in Los Angeles, I started working as a reporter. It was a three-month trial period that amounted to an intensive course in civics, local politics, and journalism in the United States. But to my great wonder and surprise, nobody told me what to say and what not to say. There was no censorship of any kind, completely unlike the state of journalism back in Mexico.

Ever since then, there have been two things that I have always admired about the United States. First, there is the tremendous freedom of the press, enshrined in the First Amendment to the Constitution (yes, the First Amendment, not the Second or Third). And second, there is the sentence in the Declaration of Independence stating that all men (and women) are created equal.

Freedom and equality.

And that was how I lived my life in the United States from the early 1980s: with absolute freedom to write and report on whatever I wanted. I was always treated fairly, despite being an immigrant with an accent.

Until Donald Trump arrived on the scene.

The Revolution Is Here

———

The United States is changing. It is growing increasingly more mixed and diverse, more multiethnic, multiracial, and multicultural. And no one, not even Trump, can change that.

The key year is 2044.

According to the Census Bureau, that is about the time when non-Hispanic whites will cease to be the majority in the United States. Everyone—white, black, Hispanic, Asian, and Native American—will be a minority. This will be a country of new faces, different accents, and many combinations of colors and origins, of food and music and art from all across the world.

The United States—the world's major economic and military power—is about to become representative of the planet as a whole, and that will require a huge dose of tolerance. This future can already be seen in elementary schools and neonatal wards in cities such as Los Angeles, Miami, and New York.

Those 2044 projections indicate that non-Hispanic whites will make up only 49.7 percent of the population, with Latinos at 25.1 percent, African Americans at 12.7 percent, Asians at 7.9 percent, and 3.7 percent for people who identify as multiracial.

There are two fundamental things to note. The first is how the non-Hispanic white population will decline from 62.2 percent in 2014 to less than 50 percent in 2044. That downtrend is expected to continue, to 44 percent by 2060.

The other important point is that the Latino and Asian populations are both expected to grow—by 115 percent and 128 percent, respectively—during the relatively short period from 2014 to 2060.

Projections indicate that Hispanics will jump from a population of 57 million in 2015 to around 100 million by 2045 and nearly 120 million by 2060.

There is no magic or witchcraft involved in America's demographic future. Whites are on the decline while Hispanics and Asians are on the rise. It's as simple as that . . . and that's what bothers some of Trump's followers.

With a bit of luck, I'll be eighty-six years old in 2044. But we won't have to wait that long to witness the changes taking place. Even as early as 2015, a majority of babies less than a year old were members of a minority. And the change is coming from below.

We are in the midst of a real demographic revolution.

It is the revolution that Cesar Chavez, the historic leader

of the Latino community, predicted. In a speech to the Commonwealth Club in San Francisco in 1984, he saw the changes that were on the horizon:

"We have looked into the future and the future is ours!" he declared. "History and inevitability are on our side. . . . These trends are part of the forces of history that cannot be stopped. No person and no organization can resist them for very long. They are inevitable. Once social change begins, it cannot be reversed. You cannot uneducate the person who has learned to read. You cannot humiliate the person who feels pride. You cannot oppress the people who are not afraid anymore."

California is living in the future. It's not exactly how Chavez would have pictured it, but on July 1, 2014, Latinos had officially outpaced non-Hispanic whites as the largest single demographic group in California. According to Census Bureau figures, there are 15 million Latinos to 14.9 million non-Hispanic whites.

But power is not proportional to population growth. While Chavez believed that the children and grandchildren of the unionized farmworkers would come to "dominate" the labor situation in the California fields (even if they didn't necessarily become landowners themselves), this has not yet happened.

But what has taken place are the demographic and generational changes and the new sense of awareness among younger Latinos that they have created. The future is theirs.

Not only will there be more of them, they will have more power as well.

Here's an example I use often: When 2018 begins, Latinos will represent 18 percent of the population. But we have only four senators. Four! We should have eighteen. We need four-teen more.

I'm not talking about quotas or formulas, just the simple fact that a people should have political representation that corresponds to its population. We don't have this yet. But that is changing, slowly but surely.

We have more congressmen than ever, more senators than ever, more governors than ever, and—for the first time in history—in 2016 we had two Latino presidential candidates in Marco Rubio and Ted Cruz.

We are gaining greater political power.

We are becoming better educated.

We are earning more money.

These are all breakthroughs. But they're not enough, nor are they happening fast enough.

And these gains are not being reflected in the media. According to the Latino Media Gap, "Stories about Latinos constitute less than 1% of news media coverage, and the majority of these stories feature Latinos as lawbreakers." In 2013, none of the top-ten rated television shows featured a Latino star, and from 2010 to 2013, Hispanics represented only 1.1 percent of the producers of these shows, 2 percent of the writers, and 4.1 percent of the directors.

The challenge is to translate increasing numbers into increasing power. And we're seeing that more and more. Tom Llamas was named the sole weekend anchor and chief national correspondent for the ABC News program *World News Tonight*, while Cecilia Vega was named senior White House correspon-dent for the Disney unit, and José Díaz-Balart was named the anchor of the Saturday edition of *NBC Nightly News*.

I am not proposing that the growing political, economic, and cultural power of Latinos be granted at the expense of any other group. It's not about excluding anyone. Rather, it is about including Latinos in the process. They are a fundamental part of the American population and have suffered from racism and discrimination for far too long.

Hatred

———

Despite all the progress we have made, we still often find ourselves on the defensive. Why is that? If we are an important part of the United States, if we are growing so quickly and gaining more political, educational, and economic power, why are there times when we feel attacked?

The answer has nothing to do with low self-esteem or psychological trauma. We feel defensive because we are literally being attacked.

There is a growing resistance to the social and demographic changes that the United States is currently undergoing, and the response by many sectors of the population has been to attack those they perceive as a threat. Trump's racist and xenophobic statements have encouraged many to overtly express their rejection of minority groups.

Sanam Malik of the Center for American Progress has expressed this idea better than anyone in her article titled "When Public Figures Normalize Hate": "Calling it a theory of 'activation,' Karen Stenner, a professor of politics at Princeton University, argues in *The Authoritarian Dynamic* that when certain people perceive a threat to the 'oneness and sameness' of their group, they can adopt riskier and more violent behaviors. Public figures and the media can certainly stoke such fear when they paint certain groups as threatening outsiders."

Hatred is contagious, and the infection is spread from top to bottom. As the scholar Francis Fukuyama wrote in a tweet, "The world is producing a bunch of mini-Trumps under the radar."

It's impossible to draw a direct line of causality between Trump's words and the bullying being experienced by minorities. But neither can we say that it's a simple coincidence.

After Trump's attacks on and criticisms of immigrants and Muslims, the number of recognized hate groups in the country increased sharply. According to the Southern Poverty Law Center, it jumped from 784 in 2014 to 917 in 2016.

The most dramatic increase was seen in anti-Muslim groups. These tripled from 34 in 2014 to 101 in 2016. During that stretch of time, there were dozens of attacks on mosques all across the country.

Additionally, groups linked to the Ku Klux Klan rose from 72 to 130 over that same period.

No one told me about this hatred.

I saw it with my own eyes.

One night, behind a house in small-town Ohio, my team

of documentarians and I watched as around twenty white supremacists nailed together a wooden swastika and set it on fire. They formed a circle around it and then, raising their right hands in a Nazi salute, began to chant, "White power! White power!"

I don't often keep my mouth shut. But there, for almost three hours—during the burning of the swastika and the racist speeches that followed—I didn't say a single word. I have a distinct accent when I speak in English, and it didn't seem safe to me (or to the other journalists and technicians who were there with me filming the documentary) to express my views in favor of diversity and tolerance at a white supremacist rally. Even less so considering that some of them were armed. The police were nowhere to be seen during the entire ceremony.

That experience reminded me of two books.

The first was James Baldwin's revealing work titled *The Fire Next Time.* First published in 1963, it describes in brutal clarity what happens when one race feels superior to another: "The glorification of one race and the consequent debasement of another—or others—always has been and always will be a recipe for murder."

The other is *A Nation of Immigrants* by former president John F. Kennedy. In his foreword, Abraham H. Foxman writes, "While racial superiority is no longer the parlance of our time, today hate groups rail against non-white immigration and urge Americans to 'fight back' against the perceived 'invasion' of the 'white' United States by Hispanics from Mexico."

When one considers Trump and many of his followers, this observation has a deeply concerning effect.

Words matter.

Trump and his followers have been looking to portray Hispanic immigrants as a danger to the United States. When Trump launched his candidacy, he said that the immigrants arriving from Mexico and the rest of Latin America were drug traffickers, criminals, and rapists. But once again, he was wrong.

I'll prove it to you. With facts and figures.

What I won't do is defend the undocumented immigrants who are real criminals. Absolutely not. It is true that a very small number of undocumented people have committed murders, rapes, armed robberies, and other violent crimes. We know this because every time a serious incident involving an undocumented immigrant occurs, the more conservative wing of the nation's media takes it upon themselves to not only cover but highlight it. The problem is that they often take the case out of context and criminalize the entire undocumented population.

This is an issue that must be treated with great care and respect. I've spoken with two parents who lost their children through incidents involving undocumented immigrants. Their pain is boundless. I listened to their stories, which were weighted with beautiful memories of their children and the terrible feeling of knowing they will never see them again. As a parent myself, I could never begin to comprehend what they must be feeling or the emptiness that now inhabits their homes.

Stepping back from the political debate, they argued that if those undocumented immigrants had never set foot in this country, their children would still be alive. And I have no defense against that argument. What I did tell them is that it does not seem right to me to persecute and vilify an entire community of millions of undocumented immigrants based on the actions of two people. Yes, there are those who have committed serious crimes, but the vast majority have not.

Still, the loss these families feel is as incalculable as it is irreparable. I'll repeat here what I said to them in person: I am sorry for their loss. Truly sorry.

So then, what are the real numbers regarding undocumented criminals? In an interview with the news program *60 Minutes*, Trump stated that "what we are going to do is get the people that are criminal and have criminal records—gang members, drug dealers, we have a lot of these people, probably two million, it could be even three million."

Where did he get these figures? Nobody knows. It appears he may have made them up, because they are ten times higher than the concrete data that exist. His tendency, after all, is to exaggerate. According to the Migration Policy Institute, only three hundred thousand undocumented immigrants have a felony conviction on their records.

That number was estimated based on data released to Congress by the Department of Homeland Security in 2012, at which time there were 11.2 million undocumented immigrants living in the United States. That means less than 2.7 percent were responsible for having committed a serious crime. And this number would be even lower if using a false Social Security number were a less serious offense. The fact of the matter is that thousands of undocumented people use them to work for U.S. companies, and their employers are fully aware of what's going on.

This may come as a surprise, but if we follow the statistics, in general undocumented immigrants conduct themselves better than many Americans. Let's do the math. According to a study conducted by Princeton University, in 2010, 8.6 percent of adult U.S. citizens had a felony conviction on their record. That's over three times the rate for undocumented immigrants.

Conclusion: over 97 percent of undocumented immigrants are good people, not the "bad hombres" described by Trump.

And there's even more data to support that.

It's no secret that the undocumented population increased dramatically from 3.5 million in 1990 to 11.2 million in 2013. But according to the FBI, during that same time frame, violent crimes fell 48 percent. This might seem incredible to many—especially if they follow the more conservative social media sites—but the reality is that there are more undocumented people here now, and crime rates have decreased.

It might seem like a joke, but what do you do if you want less crime in your cities? Bring in more immigrants.

I don't want to overwhelm you with facts, but it's important to use data to discredit the lies that Trump is perpetuating about the undocumented. Some, very few, in fact, are gang members; we're not talking about a population whose members often end up behind bars. According to a study undertaken by the Immigration Policy Center (the research and policy arm of the American Immigration Council), only 1.6 percent of immigrant men between the ages of 18 and 39 end up in prison, compared with 3.3 percent of those who were born in the United States.

So which one of us is telling the truth?

The contrast couldn't be sharper. Trump, the conservative

media, and the anti-immigrant groups present us as rapists, murderers, gang members, abusers, beaters, cheaters, counterfeiters, and criminals. But the reality is that immigrants—undocumented and otherwise—commit fewer crimes than natural-born Americans. We are supportive and generous, we help those who need it the most, and we contribute greatly to the country that accepted us.

There is, however, one other accusation: that we are thieves. People who don't pay taxes. Who are exploiting the U.S. economy, looking for free benefits without working to earn them.

Well, you may already know what I'm about to tell you, but this also is false. Don't take my word for it; look at the numbers.

There is no doubt that immigrants, both with and without papers, can be expensive. There are huge costs in the fields of education and health and social services. But what immigrants contribute far exceeds these expenses.

Undocumented workers pay taxes, create jobs, and do the work that nobody else wants to do. The question is whether they are a burden on or a benefit to the United States. To know this, we have to add up all their economic contributions and deduct from that figure their cost to society.

The National Academy of Sciences, which comprises leading scientists and researchers from across the country, ran those calculations in 2016 and published its findings in a telling report, titled *The Economic and Fiscal Consequences of Immigration*. Their conclusion: immigrants added $54.2 billion to the U.S. economy from 1994 to 2013. That's what's known as an "immigration surplus."

Immigrants contribute an average of $2 billion a year to the U.S. economy. It's a huge surplus.

And that's not all: immigrants don't steal jobs from American workers. "There is little evidence that immigration significantly affects the overall employment levels of native-born workers," the report concluded.

While the numbers aren't always a perfect match, other studies also find that immigrants add to, rather than subtract from, the economy. They pay taxes, a lot of taxes. A report by the American Immigration Council estimates that immigrants earn approximately $240 billion a year and pay $90 billion in taxes, while using only $5 billion in public benefits.

In today's age of so-called fake news, it's easy to bombard the social networks with false information about immigrants. And if someone as powerful as the president himself is the one distorting reality, promoting stereotypes, and inventing lies, it can be difficult to generate a counternarrative that contradicts the head of state. But the fact that Trump is the president doesn't mean he's right.

I know I've spent the last couple of pages hammering away at the facts and figures in the studies, but it's the only way to demonstrate that Trump's statements about immigrants are slanderous. We are not criminals, we are not rapists, and we are not a drain on the U.S. economy. We contribute more than we take, the vast majority of us are not "bad hombres" or gang members, and we are extremely grateful for all the opportunities this nation has given us.

Why does Trump attack us as much as he does? Does he truly hate immigrants, or is it just part of a political strategy, first to win the White House and later to maintain the support of his base? I don't know the answer to this.

I don't know if he's a racist at heart, but I do know that he has made racist and derogatory comments.

I'm not interested in what's going on inside Trump's head. But I do know what comes out of his mouth.

There Is No Invasion

———

After listening to a few minutes of a Trump speech, one might assume that the United States is about to be invaded or that it is facing a serious threat from the south.

But this isn't true.

Immigrants are not invading the country. Nevertheless, Trump wants to build "a big, beautiful wall" to hold back a threat that exists only in his head.

The number of undocumented immigrants in the United States has remained stable for nearly a decade. According to several studies conducted by the Pew Research Center, there were 11.3 million undocumented immigrants in 2016: exactly the same figure as in 2009. Nor is there a conspiracy among Mexicans to invade the United States and retake the territory they lost in the Mexican-American War of 1846–1848. In fact, more and more Mexicans are saying adios.

It's true: more Mexicans are leaving the United States than entering. The Pew Research Center indicates that the number of Mexicans living in the United States fell by 140,000 between 2009 and 2016. Why? Because they want to be with their families, they're uncomfortable living in the shadows and fearing U.S. Immigration and Customs Enforcement (ICE), they're no longer seeing the economic benefits of working in the United States, and the opportunities in Mexico have been improving.

That's why they're heading home. They never felt comfortable enough in the United States to make it their permanent home.

They were always strangers.

Instead of a Mexican invasion of the United States, what we're currently witnessing is the end of four decades of intense and feverish migration from south to north. Between 1965 and 2015, sixteen million Mexicans migrated to the United States. It was one of the largest migrations in the history not only of this country, but of this world.

All waves of migration are generated by two factors: one, something is pushing people out of their home nation; and two, something is attracting them to a new destination. Impoverished and underdeveloped conditions in Mexico and the rest of Latin America were the main forces driving millions of people to pack their bags and head north. But the United States is also responsible for this wave of immigration.

The undocumented immigrants are because of us.

We are all complicit.

Do you like fruit? You might be wondering what this has to do with what we're talking about. A lot, as it turns out. We wouldn't have fruit available at reasonable prices if it weren't for the work of thousands of undocumented immigrants. The strawberries, apples, and grapes that you like so much made their way from field to table thanks to the invisible work of people who do not have permission to work here.

Agriculture—as well as the service industry, from hotels to restaurants—depends on unauthorized workers. The next time you go to a restaurant, take a peek into the kitchen. Chances are that it's full of undocumented workers, regardless of the cuisine being served. You can claim that you don't condone the presence of people who arrived in this country illegally, but every time you buy a piece of fruit, dine at a restaurant, or check into a hotel, you're indirectly supporting them with your wallet.

Nothing has done more to encourage Mexicans and other Latin Americans to come to the United States than the Immigration and Nationality Act of 1965, which was inspired by the words of President John F. Kennedy. This law ended the system of national quotas—which gave an advantage to European immigrants—and instead emphasized bringing in talented people and unifying families.

In an effort to end official discrimination, Kennedy proposed changing immigration laws in an address to Congress on July 23, 1963. The purpose of this bill was to develop an immigration law "that serves the national interest and reflects in every detail the principles of equality and human dignity to which our nation subscribes." Kennedy was assassinated on November 22 of that same year, but his ideas lived on, and the new law was passed in 1965.

The results of this change have been clear. Most of the immigrants who arrived in the nineteenth and early twentieth centuries came from Ireland, Italy, Poland, and other European nations. But since 1965, roughly half of all new immigrants have come from Latin America, while a quarter stem from Asia. And as a result, the United States has undergone a demographic transformation.

This explains the Mexican wave. But that wave has already crested. In 2013, for example, immigrants from China (147,000) and India (129,000) outnumbered immigrants from Mexico (125,000), according to a *Wall Street Journal* report.

This is what Trump doesn't understand. He wants a wall—an absurd and expensive wall—to halt an invasion that exists only in his imagination. But such a wall would become Trump's white elephant: a massive construction, highly visible and yet totally useless.

A Useless Wall

———

L et's look at the geography of stupidity.

Mexico and the United States share a border 1,954 miles long. Some sort of wall or fencing already exists along roughly 700 miles of it. Theoretically, these physical barriers would have to be extended at least another 1,200 miles, which would be a stratospheric waste of time and money.

Donald Trump loves to remind us that he is very intelligent and that he is a great businessman. But if that is true, then why build an incredibly expensive structure that will not stop the flow of either immigrants or drugs?

According to a Pew Research Center study, about 45 percent of all undocumented immigrants in the United States arrive by plane and then overstay their visas. In other words, no matter how long or how high the wall is, it will have no effect on nearly half of immigrants, who will remain here illegally.

Supposedly, the wall would protect U.S. cities along the border with Mexico. But it turns out that these communities are already some of the safest in the entire country. An investigation conducted by *The Texas Tribune*, published on February 23, 2016, found that "border communities have lower crime rates."

In 2014, border towns such as Laredo, Brownsville, and El Paso reported fewer than four hundred crimes per one hundred thousand people. "It's much safer than say San Antonio, Houston or Dallas," state senator Juan "Chuy" Hinojosa said in that same report. "It's certainly much safer than Washington D.C. or Chicago." For comparison's sake, Houston and Dallas reported 991 and 665 crimes, respectively, per 100,000 people during that same period.

And the same thing is taking place in Arizona. In public testimony given on September 13, 2013, Sheriff Tony Estrada said that Santa Cruz County, which borders Nogales, Mexico, "is a very safe, very secure area." And this is despite the fact that at least one hundred tunnels for smuggling drugs and undocumented workers had been discovered connecting Nogales, Arizona (located in Santa Cruz County), with Nogales, Mexico.

Nor will the wall stop drugs from flowing into the United States.

This is something that many Americans may not want to hear, but it has to be said nonetheless. As long as millions of them are using drugs, there will be drug traffickers in Mexico and the rest of Latin America ready to manufacture them and ship them north. When the demand is this high, no wall will stop the drug dealers, who are always looking for ever more creative ways to get narcotics across the border.

Here are the disturbing facts: In 2013, 24.6 million Americans admitted to having used some type of drug during the previous month, according to the National Institute on Drug Abuse.

As long as there are customers to support it, narcotrafficking will continue to be an unstoppable force. Joaquín "El Chapo" Guzmán, the word's most prolific smuggler, is now in a New York prison. But he is already being replaced by a new generation of drug lords. When one tree is chopped down, others will sprout up in its place.

And if we were somehow wrong and Trump's multibillion-dollar wall could stop the flow of immigrants and drugs, traffickers would find new covert routes by sea, as Cuban refugees with their makeshift boats have skillfully and courageously demonstrated for years now. Yes, all nations have the right to clear and secure borders. But in the case of the border between Mexico and the United States—a "scar," as the writer Carlos Fuentes once described it—the solution isn't a wall, but rather a multinational relationship that manages, protects, and stimulates legal immigration. If Latin America has workers and the United States needs them to fill in for an aging population, why not create a system of migration that works not only for North America but also for the rest of the continent?

Nobody wants illegal immigration, not even undocumented immigrants. We can all agree on this. It is dangerous, unmanageable, and controlled by people outside of the two respective governments. This is why we have to look for safe and effective alternatives.

Creating an insurmountable wall is an extremely foolhardy idea for solving a complex international problem. This one will require a much more creative solution. Let's be frank here: extending the existing wall between Mexico and the United States is impractical—especially considering the daunting engineering challenges and the cumbersome issues of land and water rights—and its proposal has created some of the sharpest clashes in decades between two friendly nations.

Plus, it's impossibly expensive.

And Mexico is not going to pay for it.

Let's say you want to build a fence around your yard, and suddenly you have the idea that you can force your neighbor to pay for it. I know, it sounds ridiculous. But that's exactly what Donald Trump wants Mexico to do.

When Trump announced this outlandish idea back in the summer of 2015, the Mexican government should have stated outright that it would not contribute one cent to constructing the wall. But it didn't.

In the wake of the Mexican government's complicit silence, only former president Vicente Fox was willing to speak up. "I'm not going to pay for that fucking wall," he told me in a February 2016 interview. "He should pay for it."

In August of that same year, at a fateful press conference in Mexico City, Mexican president Enrique Peña Nieto had the chance to tell Trump "no" to his face. But he didn't dare. Be that as it may, Trump's wall will end up being paid for by Americans, not Mexicans.

Many estimates have been made. One, by Senate Majority

Leader Mitch McConnell, put the cost at somewhere between $12 billion and $15 billion, maybe more. But worst of all, it won't do anything.

If Trump truly understood the demographic changes the United States is experiencing, he would be looking east instead of south. Because after the Latino wave comes the Asian wave.

Despite Trump's xenophobic efforts, immigrants will continue to arrive on these shores. Not so many from Mexico and the rest of Latin America, but more from Asian nations going forward.

The tide has always been rising.

Accepting foreigners has always been an American tradition.

As the late John F. Kennedy reminds us in *A Nation of Immigrants*, in 1820 there were barely 150,000 immigrants in the United States. But by 1840 that number had jumped to 1.7 million; by 1880 it reached 5.2 million; and in 1910 the total reached 8.8 million. The influx of immigrants has never stopped.

According to a visionary study by the Pew Research Center, over the past fifty years—from 1965 to 2015—the number of foreigners living in the United States has increased from 9.6 million to 45 million. And in the next fifty years, that figure is expected to increase to 78 million. To put it another way, foreigners in the United States will be increasing from 14 percent to nearly 18 percent of the total population.

The year 2055 will mark the beginning of the Asian era in the United States. That year, immigrants from Asian countries—China, India, Korea, Vietnam, and the Philippines among them—will surpass those from Latin American nations.

It's going to be a real demographic tsunami.

And it will require huge amounts of tolerance and cooperation. Just as Donald Trump is attacking Latin American immigrants today, I would not be surprised if a future presidential candidate decided to attack Asian immigrants to win votes.

Of course, you can't block off China with a wall, as Trump is proposing to do with Mexico, but terrible examples from history could resurface. For example, in 1882 Congress passed the Chinese Exclusion Act, which was designed to prevent Chinese laborers from immigrating to the United States, particularly California, and allowed people to openly discriminate against those who were already here. This injustice was not corrected until 1943.

More Asian immigrants will be appearing on the horizon.

The fact of the matter is that during the next half century, we will be adding roughly six hundred thousand immigrants per year. That is why it is so urgent to have a new immigration system in place, so that we can process the immigrants who are already here, along with the millions who have yet to come.

There are no excuses. We have been warned, and we must be prepared. The Asian wave is coming. Meanwhile, Trump is banging his head against his wall.

No One Is Illegal

———

"Illegals."

That's what they call them.

As Holocaust survivor and Nobel Peace Prize laureate Elie Wiesel once said, "No human being is illegal." A person may commit an illegal act, but nobody can be illegal in and of himself.

This term has become so widespread in the United States that even some of the more liberal politicians and members of the media are using it. Democrats I have interviewed are generally confused and apologetic when they use the word "illegal" to refer to an undocumented immigrant, and they correct themselves. But almost every Republican I have spoken with uses the term without any sense of regret or consequence.

The term "illegal" has come to refer almost exclusively

to immigrants from Latin America. As Roberto Suro, a researcher and professor at the University of Southern California, wrote in his extraordinary book *Strangers Among Us*, "No immigrant group has carried the stigma of illegality that now attaches itself to many Latinos." Why? Because "no industrialized nation has ever faced such a vast migration across a land border with the virtual certainty that it will continue to challenge the government's ability to control that border for years to come."

"Illegal" is used to refer to people who don't have their papers in order, but it is never applied to the people or companies who hire them. Never have I heard someone say, "This is an illegal enterprise by the simple fact that it employs undocumented people." It's a complete double standard.

This is doubtless seen as a triumph for those who insist on dehumanizing the undocumented. It is much easier to attack, detain, abuse, and deport someone you consider "illegal" than it is a person whose face you recognize, whose name you know, and who resides in this country legally.

To call someone "illegal" is to strip that person of humanity and establish different degrees of false superiority among equal human beings. There are many other ways of doing this.

Throughout my career, I have spoken with dozens of people who have experienced the deportation of a family member. This is a devastating experience for them. Out of nowhere, an ICE agent appears at an undocumented immigrant's home or place of work, and within a matter of minutes, that person is arrested, booked, and on the way to being deported. When this sort of thing happens in plain view of children or other minors, it can have a traumatic impact and leave permanent psychological scars.

Video footage of these arrests almost always includes scenes of desperate children crying, "What are they doing to my mom?" or, "Where are they taking my dad?" They have no way to understand why someone who has spent his or her entire life working for the well-being of the family would suddenly end up detained and subjected to deportation proceedings.

When something like this happens, cruel comments on social networks can be surprising, even going so far as to suggest that undocumented immigrants deserve this sort of treatment because they came to the United States illegally and put their children and families in this situation. These sorts of criticisms can be made much more easily when the incumbent president and his administration are constantly reinforcing the narrative that undocumented immigrants are criminals and "illegals."

Being "illegal" is much, much harder than being a stranger.

I recently traveled to Los Angeles to meet Fátima, an American-born fourteen-year-old with three American sisters. One morning in early 2017, Fátima's father, Rómulo Avélica, was taking her to school. But shortly before they arrived, he was detained by ICE agents. Rómulo is from the Mexican state of Nayarit and illegally immigrated to the United States over twenty years ago.

The agents forced him out of his car and arrested him right in front of Fátima's eyes . . . and in front of her cell phone. The video, complete with her cries and pleas, went viral on social media.

"He's not a criminal," Fátima told me. "He's just a dad."

During our interview, she took me to the exact spot where her father was arrested, just a few blocks away from her school. Clearly, the ICE agents had been following them. Fátima couldn't stay there long, for memories of her father's arrest soon brought tears to her eyes. It was clear that she was carrying a deep sense of anguish and grief inside her.

Rómulo had previously been arrested for a traffic violation and driving under the influence. He was also under a pending deportation order, but he never expected to be arrested with his daughter in the car on the way to school.

The life of Rómulo's wife and four daughters had taken an unexpected turn. In addition to the emotional trauma, they lost their family's primary source of income and had to take on numerous extra expenses to pay for Rómulo's legal defense while he was detained in a facility two hours away.

The arrest of a single undocumented immigrant can destroy an entire family's life. And Fátima's family isn't the only one.

Guadalupe García de Rayos is considered to be the first undocumented immigrant to be deported during Trump's presidency. That's impossible to confirm, but the pain is not.

Guadalupe was brought here by her parents from Guanajuato, Mexico, when she was just fourteen years old. Her husband also came, without documents, when he was a child. He said to me, "We, my wife and I, did not make the decision to come to this country. We were minors. This is where we met. This is where we got married. This is where we go to church on Sundays. We live a normal life. Just like any Anglo-Saxon person with his papers in order. Documents don't define what kind of a person you are."

Nevertheless, Guadalupe was deported for lacking them.

She was arrested in a raid during the fearsome era of Sheriff Joe Arpaio in Maricopa County, Arizona, and charged with using a false Social Security number. When I interviewed her, she explained that she didn't steal it from anyone; she simply made it up so that she could work.

During the administration of President Barack Obama, Guadalupe would not have been a deportation priority. At that time, the fundamental intent was to deport people who had committed serious crimes, who had just recently entered the United States, or who had attempted to enter illegally on many occasions. Guadalupe lived her life without any major setbacks. Once a year she had to go to an ICE office in Phoenix and prove that she hadn't been in any trouble with the law. She did this for eight years.

One morning in February 2017, less than a month after Trump was sworn in as president, Guadalupe went to her annual interview with ICE. But this time, things changed. After her interview, she was arrested and informed that she would be deported back to Mexico, a country where she hadn't lived for twenty-two years.

Her children, Jacqueline, fourteen, and Ángel, sixteen, were confused and inconsolable. What was different this time? Deportation policies under a new White House administration. New arrivals and people with a criminal background would no longer be the primary targets for deportations. Virtually all undocumented people of legal age were at risk.

In early 2017, the *Los Angeles Times* estimated that out of the eleven million undocumented immigrants living in this country, as many as eight million could be subject to deportation under the new priorities established by Trump's presidency.

Guadalupe was one of the first. Perhaps the immigration agents wanted to use her as an example for the rest of the Hispanic community. But the effect on the García de Rayos family was horrific.

"Nobody should ever have to pack her mother's suitcase." This is what Guadalupe's daughter, Jacqueline, said during an impromptu press conference held after learning that her mother was to be deported. "It's very hard for me," she explained, "not knowing if I'll ever be able to see her face-to-face again, to give her a hug or a kiss."

Indeed. Nobody should ever have to pack up her mother's belongings. But Jacqueline did. Guadalupe was sent back to Mexico through the border town of Nogales, Arizona. "First I was a victim of Arpaio," she said as she crossed over. "And now I'm a victim of Trump."

"It was a devastating blow," her husband said. "No child should ever have to pack up her mother's things. There is no justice in these laws. They're playing dirty with us."

With Trump in the White House, the anti-immigrant climate in the United States has changed for the worse. There are frequent verbal attacks on foreigners, coupled with the perception that any undocumented person can be deported at any time, regardless of past compliance. Further, several local police forces, operating with the explicit support of their respective mayors, have begun to act like ICE agents.

The sense of fear is palpable.

Obama: Deporter in Chief

———

My animosity toward, annoyance at, and rejection of Donald Trump's words and attitude regarding immigrants is clear. But this is not a partisan issue. I am registered in the United States as an independent voter and have never publicly or financially supported any political party. I have criticized Republicans and Democrats alike.

And Barack Obama was no exception.

President Obama earned the title "deporter in chief." It was given to him by Janet Murguía, president of UnidosUS (formerly the National Council of La Raza), and the president was never able to shed it.

I have here in front of me the statistics on deportations during the Obama presidency. They're not pretty. In fact, they're painful. According to official ICE data, from 2009 through 2016—Obama's term in office—2,749,706 people were deported.

He deported more immigrants than any other president in history.

It can be difficult to criticize President Obama because he has always been in favor of immigration reform and because he protected hundreds of thousands of Dreamers from deportation. But the fact is that he needlessly destroyed thousands of Hispanic families.

If his strategy was to show that he was in full compliance with immigration laws in order to convince a Republican-controlled Congress to approve comprehensive immigration reform, it failed. Republicans never showed any real interest in cooperating with the Obama administration on immigration issues. Meanwhile, thousands of people with no criminal record were ripped from their families and deported.

Obama was also wrong not to take advantage of his first few months in office—when Democrats controlled not only the White House but also both chambers of Congress—to pass comprehensive immigration reform, as he had promised to do during his campaign.

I've told this story many times. On May 28, 2008, during his first presidential campaign, I interviewed him at a school in Denver, Colorado. His opponent, Hillary Clinton, had said that if she was elected, she would present a proposal for immigration reform to Congress within her first one hundred days in office. I asked Obama if he would do the same, and he said no.

But then he promised the following: "What I can guarantee

is that we will have in the first year [of the presidency] an immigration bill that I strongly support. . . ."

"In the first year?" I insisted.

"In the first year," he repeated.

It never happened.

Obama's unfulfilled promise is one of the greatest frustrations the Latino community has with our former president. And I let him know this on a number of occasions.

Once, during a community forum in 2012 and deep in the midst of his reelection campaign, I told Obama that he had failed us. "You promised that," I said. "A promise is a promise. And with all due respect, you didn't keep that promise."

By then it was too late. Obama and the Democrats had lost control of the House of Representatives. No bill was going to move through there.

Our first mistake, I realize now, was to believe in a political promise and to not do enough to make sure Obama followed through on it. It was a serious case of naïveté, one that came at a huge, tangible cost to the lives of many immigrant families.

What bothers me the most is that it was a political decision. I have since had many conversations with members of his administration, and my only conclusion is that someone inside the White House convinced him not to push for immigration reform in 2009. Until the passing of Senator Ted Kennedy on August 25, 2009, Democrats controlled both chambers of Congress.

Rahm Emanuel was Barack Obama's chief of staff at the time.

"So what happened that first year?" I asked him. "Why didn't he present immigration reform as he had promised? You were there."

"As you know, Jorge, in his first year he had a massive economy, that was a recession, that was going towards a depression. That was his first attention. It was what he focused on, number one," Emanuel replied.

Janet Napolitano was secretary of homeland security during that same period of time.

"In 2009 you were in charge of the immigration department," I said to her during a 2013 interview. "Why is it that President Barack Obama didn't move on immigration reform as he promised during the campaign? What happened?"

"Well, I think what happened is he took over the presidency at a time when we were on a cliff to going into a great depression," she replied, before going on to add, "We were involved in wars in Afghanistan and Iraq. I mean, he acquired a lot."

To me, the explanations provided by Emanuel and Napolitano were nothing more than excuses. Nothing could explain Obama's inaction or his terrible political decision to wait.

I understand that there were other priorities. The United States went through one of the worst economic crises in modern history. But aren't we able to confront more than one challenge at a time? Someone made the decision to push immigration to the side. I don't know if it was the president himself or one of his senior advisers, but regardless, in the end Obama made the decision.

Everyone knew that the president had made a promise on immigration reform, and everyone knows that—whether for political or strategic reasons—he decided to break that promise. I suspect the administration thought that Latinos would be willing to wait a little bit longer and that the cost of postponing it would not be too great.

And, sadly, we let it happen. To ourselves. We didn't speak up loudly enough.

We were passed over.

Yet again.

On December 9, 2014, I had one final fight with Obama. By that time, there was nothing that could be done on immigration reform. The Republicans were never going to cooperate, yet the president was continuing to deport thousands of undocumented immigrants. Why?

Back then, the president had just announced an executive action, the Deferred Action for Childhood Arrivals (DACA), designed to protect hundreds of thousands of young, undocumented immigrants known as Dreamers who were brought to the United States as minors by their parents. It was the single most important immigration decision of his entire presidency. He was truly changing lives.

But if the president had come to the conclusion that he could either stop, postpone, or suspend the deportation of the Dreamers, why couldn't he do the same for other immigrants? I asked him this, and our exchange was extremely tense:

"If you, as you were saying, always had the legal authority to stop deportations, then why did you deport two million people?" I asked.

"Jorge, we're not going to—"

"For six years you did."

"No, listen, Jorge—"

"You destroyed many families. They called you 'deporter in chief.'"

"You called me 'deporter in chief.'"

"It was Janet Murguía from La Raza."

"Yeah, but let me say this, Jorge—"

"Well, you haven't stopped deportations."

"No, no, no."

"That's the whole idea."

"That's not true. Listen, here's the facts of the matter—"

"You could have stopped them."

"Jorge, here's the facts of the matter. As president of the United States, I'm always responsible for problems that aren't solved right away. . . . The question is, are we doing the right thing, and have we consistently tried to move this country in a better direction? And those, like you sometimes, Jorge, who suggest that there are simple, quick answers to these problems, I think—"

"I didn't say that."

"Yes, you do, because that's how you present it."

"But you had the authority."

"When you present it that way, it does a disservice. Because it makes the assumption that the political process is one that can easily be moved around, depending on the will of one person. And that's not how things work—"

"What I'm saying is—"

"We spent that entire time trying to get a comprehensive immigration reform bill done that would solve the problem for all the people. So right now, by the actions that I've taken, I still have five million people who do not have the ability to register and be confident that they are not deported."

———

That was my final conversation with Barack Obama. He did not agree to speak with me during the rest of his time in office. I learned from people close to him that he was annoyed by my continued insistence on the subject of deportations—how could we let that go?—and because we did not see the issue of repatriation in the same way.

He insisted that the majority of the deportations involved people who had just recently crossed into the United States, who were living very close to the border, and, from immigrants inside the country, who had committed crimes. That much is true. But in 2016, to give you an example, only 58 percent of all deportees had committed a crime. And many times, these were minor offenses such as traffic violations or were inherently tied to their status as undocumented individuals, such as having false identification or trying to enter the United States illegally on multiple occasions.

Obama clearly deported thousands of people who were not criminals. Period. I understand that his intention—and his administration's priority—was to focus on the criminals, but ultimately that's not what happened.

The figures on deportation don't come from me. Let me give you one more example. The Migration Policy Institute concluded in 2012 that out of the approximately eleven million people living in the country illegally, only 300,000 had committed a felony. But that same year, Obama deported 409,849 of them.

Something doesn't compute. Obama was absolutely deporting people who had committed no serious crimes, and he was doing so at a very high rate. Was it legal? Yes, it was legal. But as president—and as he demonstrated by signing the executive order known as DACA—he had the authority to suspend most if not all deportations of people who were not a risk to national security. Yet he chose not to do so.

I don't know whether it was owing to a sense of guilt, the pressure he felt from Latino organizations, or a tacit acknowledgment that he had been wrong, but nearing the end of his second term in office, Obama reduced the number of deportees by nearly half: from 409,000 at its peak to 240,000 in his final year of governance.

We can debate the president's numbers and his motivations until we're out of breath, but the effects on thousands of American families were devastating. Never before had a president deported so many people.

That's why so many people have told me that we were not sufficiently tough with Obama. And maybe they're right. With the notable exception of the Dreamers, his policies were very harmful to immigrant families. Plus, he never lived up to a campaign promise that—had it been fulfilled—would have averted the state of panic under which millions of people are now living with Trump in the White House.

So why did the Latino community give Obama a gentler treatment compared with the way we're currently dealing with Trump? First and foremost, Obama never insulted us. Trump did so on the day he launched his campaign. Obama talked about inclusion while Trump tries to exclude us. Obama supported legalization and a path to citizenship for most of the eleven million undocumented immigrants in this country, while Trump does not. Obama fought for what most

Latinos want when it comes to immigration—just look at the polls—while Trump opposes them.

In politics, perceptions translate into votes. Obama won 67 and 71 percent of the Latino vote in the 2008 and 2012 elections, respectively. In 2016, Trump garnered only 29 percent.

Still, Obama's deportations continue to hurt. Perhaps it's because we expected so much from him, and he didn't deliver. Or maybe it's because it hurts even more when someone close to you kicks you out of your own home.

Our 2016 Mistake

———

What happened to the Latinos during the 2016 presidential elections that resulted in a victory for Trump?

The worst thing of all: they didn't go out to vote. More than half of them stayed home and let others make the decision for them.

What happens in the Latino community is our own fault.

It can't be blamed on anyone else.

In 2016, there were 27.3 million Latinos who were eligible to vote. It's always a new record, of course, because every year an average of 800,000 young Hispanics reach the voting age of eighteen. It's no surprise that nearly half—44 percent—of all Latino voters are millennials.

But the tragedy is that, according to the Census Bureau,

only 47.6 percent of those eligible voters—12.7 million—came out to vote in 2016. This number is slightly down from the 48 percent who voted in the 2012 election.

Latinos lost in every electoral matchup. The general public turned out in a higher percentage (61.4 percent), as did non-Hispanic whites (65.3 percent), African Americans (59.6 percent), and Asian Americans (49.3 percent).

Many Latinos complain about Donald Trump's words and policies. But 14.6 million of those who were eligible to vote chose not to. That's their fault.

If more Latinos had turned out to vote, would the end result of the presidential election have been any different? We can never know. But we won't lose anything if we crunch some of the data.

Trump won both Florida and Arizona. But a greater turnout in those two states—both of which have a large Latino population—could have kept a total of 40 electoral votes out of the Republican candidate's camp, thus preventing him from reaching the 270 needed to win.

This is, of course, pure speculation. Trump won, and half of the Latino community did not get out and vote. That's the fact of the matter.

In the wake of Trump's insults directed at Latin American immigrants during the presidential campaign, polls showed clear feelings of disgust and rejection. Trump claimed that Latinos loved him. That couldn't have been further from the truth.

The America's Voice organization published a press release titled "No, Mr. Trump, the Latinos Do Not Love You," citing several surveys that didn't support Trump's claim.

According to a September 2015 *Washington Post*/ABC News poll, 82 percent of Latinos held an unfavorable opinion of Trump. And that didn't change much over the course of the next year: according to a September 2016 *Wall Street Journal*/NBC News poll, 78 percent of Hispanics still had a negative opinion of Trump. Several other polls showed similar results.

Things were looking bad for Trump. History has shown us that if a Republican candidate fails to earn a third of the Latino vote, he or she stands a good chance of losing the general election. John McCain earned 31 percent in 2008 and lost. Mitt Romney's support dropped to 27 percent in 2012, and he lost as well. In contrast, George W. Bush gained 35 percent of the Latino vote in 2000 and 44 percent in 2004 and won both times.

That is why I said, so many times and with such great confidence, that Trump would never make it to the White House without the Latino vote.

But I was wrong.

What I didn't see was the enormous resentment that was growing among many voters regarding the country's economic situation. I believed in the majority of polls that showed Trump falling behind. And never would I have imagined that 29 percent of Latinos would vote for this particular Republican candidate.

(This 29 percent figure comes from exit polls conducted on Election Day, November 8, 2016, but several organizations have questioned their validity and suggested that the actual number is significantly lower.)

Considering his insults about Hispanic immigrants, his plans to deport millions of people during his first two years in office, and his promise to build a wall along the border with Mexico, it seemed to me all but impossible that Trump could eclipse Mitt Romney's numbers from four years earlier. But among a certain, almost secret, segment of the Latino population, support for Trump was brewing.

We have to admit that many Latinos were not comfortable openly admitting their intentions to vote for Trump. Such a statement would predictably result in harsh attacks against the candidate as well as the supporter who said such a thing. Trump generates extreme reactions across the board, and that, I believe, kept Trump's potential support among Latinos as hidden as it was silent.

Still, though, the votes were there.

I work in an office building in Miami that shares space with a number of radio and television stations. Every day I walk past the Spanish-language broadcasts, and I often stop and listen for a minute to what they're saying. Open mike and call-in programs are extremely popular, and on a number of occasions, back in 2016, I overheard listeners say—often anonymously—that they were going to vote for Trump.

I figured that those Spanish-speaking voters supporting Trump could not be statistically significant. But multimedia surveys say otherwise. And that was my mistake. I should have given more weight to those opinions.

Of course Hispanics are not a monolithic group, and of course Trump would have many Hispanic backers. For many of them, immigration reform was not their primary issue, as is the case with Cubans and Puerto Ricans. They had other concerns.

Of course there are also huge generational differences. Hispanics who have lived here for a long time, or whose families span two or three generations, can have very different viewpoints from those of newcomers. The opinions of Latinos in the Northeast and in California don't necessarily match those of Latinos in Texas and Florida. And Trump's offensive remarks about Mexicans clearly weren't game changers for the 3,640,000 Hispanics who voted for him.

There are many things Latinos can learn from past presidential elections. But the most important one is that if we don't vote, someone else will do it for us. That's exactly what happened in 2016.

Another lesson is that Trump was able to win the White House with less than a third of the Latino vote. I thought we had more influence. Not quite yet.

I personally overestimated the importance of the Latino vote. I said on numerous occasions that nobody could win the presidency without a significant portion of the Latino vote, yet Trump did it. I got ahead of myself, and this will teach me to be more careful in the future.

Eventually, of course, there will come a time when no candidate can reach the presidency without the Latino vote. But for now, if an election can be decided in states such as Pennsylvania, Michigan, and Wisconsin—places that have relatively low Hispanic populations—then our influence is diluted.

In spite of all that, I still believe that Republicans made a serious mistake with Latinos in 2016, one from which they will not easily recover. It may even end up as one of those historical blunders that becomes so legendary, it will be hard to pin down exactly how and when it began.

So let's do that here: it was when the Republican Party as a whole attached itself to Trump, a candidate with racist beliefs. What happens when you don't distance yourself from a candidate who defines the fastest-growing group of voters in the country as criminals and racists? They will forever be reminding you of it to your face.

Historically, Democrats have controlled two-thirds of the Latino vote in presidential elections. Why? Because Democrats' views on immigration issues, public education, and social policies that help those in need have been more attractive to most Hispanic voters than free-market principles and harsh enforcement of Republican immigration laws. The reasoning goes more or less like this: I'll vote for the one who helps me, who protects me, who thinks of me before him- or herself.

But that is not a captive, immutable vote.

George W. Bush won more than 40 percent of the Hispanic vote during his reelection campaign. Then, many people believed that the Latino vote could be divided equally between the two major political parties. Long before that, Ronald Reagan famously quipped that "Latinos are Republican. They just don't know it yet." And in 2004, the Republicans thought it was finally coming true.

There are certain issues on which Hispanics tend to be very conservative. According to the Pew Research Center, just over half (51 percent) believe that abortion should be illegal in all cases, compared with 41 percent of the general population. And 69 percent of Latino immigrants say religion is very important to their lives, compared with 58 percent of Americans as a whole.

And there's more. Many Latin Americans left their home

nations because of violence, corruption, and a lack of opportunity. They are often suspicious of their governments and distrustful of politicians, which is why the Republican cornerstone of smaller government is so attractive to so many.

Meritocracy goes hand in hand with three out of four Hispanics, who believe that hard work generates social progress and personal benefits. Republicans could promote all of these ideas as a way of reaching out to Latino voters.

But they still face a serious problem: How do you ask people to vote for you after you've insulted them? How do you gain people's trust if you are constantly telling them that you want to deport their parents, neighbors, and coworkers?

That was Mitt Romney's problem during the 2012 election. He wanted the Latino vote, but at the same time he promoted the idea of "self-deportation" for the undocumented. The party did so poorly with Hispanics during that election that the Republican National Committee wrote an "autopsy report" so they wouldn't make the same mistakes in the future.

Here are two of its recommendations:

"Among the steps Republicans take in the Hispanic community and beyond, we must embrace and champion comprehensive immigration reform. If we do not, our Party's appeal will continue to shrink to its core constituencies only."

"If Hispanic Americans perceive that a GOP nominee or candidate does not want them in the United States (i.e., self-deportation), they will not pay attention to our next sentence."

Exactly.

But the Republicans did not learn from their mistakes in 2012. Instead of following their own recommendations, they took an even stronger anti-immigrant stance in 2016. Their proposals? Build a wall. Massive deportations. No immigration reform. No legalization of undocumented immigrants. Ban Muslims from entering the country.

Again: If Latinos are being made to feel unwelcome by Republicans, how can they be expected to vote for Republican candidates?

This wasn't just Trump's attitude. Other Republican presidential candidates also launched harsh attacks against immigrants and minorities. The great irony is that many of them were the children of immigrants themselves.

I personally believe that the children of immigrants have two sets of responsibilities: first to care for their parents; and second to protect other immigrants as if they were their own children. This has been a noble American tradition for more than two centuries. There is nothing quite so sad and treacherous as wanting to slam the door in the face of the immigrants who come after us. But that's exactly what some presidential candidates did in 2016.

First, the good news: Never before have we seen so many children of immigrants seeking the White House. That speaks very well of our nation. In a single generation, you can go from being the son of an immigrant to president of the United States.

Here they are: Donald Trump, whose mother was born in Scotland; Marco Rubio, whose father and mother were born in Cuba; Ted Cruz, who was born in Canada to a Cuban father; Bobby Jindal, whose parents were born in India; and the independent/Democrat Bernie Sanders, whose father was from Poland.

All of them had firsthand experience of what it is like to grow up in a home marked by different accents and where at least one parent was learning the laws and customs of their adoptive country. But what struck me the most was that despite having so many children of immigrants among the presidential candidates, the overall campaign was marked by harsh attacks on immigrants themselves.

Suffice it to say that almost every one of these candidates had called undocumented immigrants "illegals" at one point. But incomprehensible to many Hispanics were the anti-immigrant positions taken by the two Latino candidates: Cuban American senators Marco Rubio and Ted Cruz.

They broke a decades-old trend in which Hispanic politicians at the national level and regardless of origin always defended the rights of the most vulnerable immigrants. Why not give this new generation of immigrants the same opportunities their parents had enjoyed?

Look, for example, at the undocumented Puerto Rican Democrats Luis Gutiérrez and Nydia Velázquez and the Cuban American Republicans Ileana Ros-Lehtinen and Lincoln and Mario Díaz-Balart.

Immigrants never forget those who help us. Ever.

The United States has been extraordinarily generous to me, and for that very reason, I argue and fight on behalf of the immigrants who came after me, so that they might have the same opportunities I did and so that they are treated with the same respect I received. That's why I don't understand why immigrants or their children would attack someone who got here just a little bit later than they did.

There is no greater show of disloyalty than when the children of immigrants are so ungrateful as to forget where they came from. It's almost a betrayal.

Trump is the son of a Scottish mother. He had a German

grandfather, and he is married to a woman from Slovenia. Four of his five children have an immigrant mother. And I cannot think of a candidate who is more anti-immigrant than he is.

The Republicans are running the risk of driving away Hispanic voters for generations to come. The results of recent elections may lead them to believe that attacking immigrants will generate more and more votes going forward. But that's not how I see it. The Trump phenomenon is unrepeatable, and tying yourself to that brand is going to cost you many future elections.

The future of the United States holds more Latinos than ever before. And there is no way to earn their support if you make them feel like strangers.

Fear and Dreamers

———

So here we are: with Trump, with no immigration reform, and with a lot of fear.

Politicians who reject a path to citizenship for millions of undocumented immigrants are not representing the wishes of a majority of Americans.

As early as 2015, the Pew Research Center concluded that 72 percent of respondents believed there should be a way to allow undocumented immigrants to remain in the country if they meet certain requirements. That's 80 percent of Democrats and 56 percent of Republicans, when split by party. Other more recent polls back up these findings.

But what the polls show is one thing. What's actually happening is something very different. Instances of a growing anti-immigrant climate—and the fear that this creates—are palpable, and they precede Trump's arrival on the political scene.

The year 2015 was particularly violent for at least three Latino immigrants, and the violence came from the police.

Here's what happened:

On February 10, police in Pasco, Washington, killed a Mexican man by the name of Antonio Zambrano-Montes after the homeless man threw rocks at them, a video shows.

On February 20, police in Grapevine, Texas, killed a Mexican man by the name of Rubén García Villalpando after a chase. According to his brother-in-law's version of events, García had his hands raised and asked one of the officers, "Are you going to kill me?" Shortly thereafter, he was shot twice in the chest.

On February 27, police in Santa Ana, California, killed a Mexican man by the name of Ernesto Canepa, who was suspected of robbery and found with a BB gun in his car. The Canepa family says he worked two jobs to support his four children.

The Mexican government sent a letter of protest to Washington officials stating concerns that these were not isolated incidents. But it did not want these three deaths to become a central issue that would strain bilateral relations.

Mexicans living in the United States are alone. They know that they are not a priority for the government in Mexico City. And when they are the target of police in the United States, they have practically no way to defend themselves.

Mexicans are killed and nothing happens.

To these three cases, we must add a dozen others involving Mexicans who clashed with U.S. Border Patrol officers since 2010, according to figures from the Southern Border Communities Coalition. The sad reality is that most of these deaths go unreported, and we almost never find out what actually happened. Law enforcement officials have virtually total impunity. There are almost never any charges brought, nor is there any real expectation of justice.

This sense of injustice for immigrants in the United States is reinforced by the language used by many politicians, both in Washington and around the country, who call them "criminals." Some are even guilty of perpetuating this false stereotype of the "criminal alien." But simply being in this country illegally is entirely different from committing a crime here.

Despite what the Declaration of Independence says, not all people here in the United States are treated as equals. Some— those who were born abroad, who speak with an accent, or who have a darker skin color than others—can lose their lives at the hands of those who are sworn to protect them: the police.

The fear is growing. Fear of being killed. Fear of being abused. Fear of being deported.

But is there a way to measure it?

Many undocumented people who, following the example set by the Dreamers, came out of the closet during Barack Obama's presidency have gone back into the shadows since Trump took office. They don't trust the police. They don't want to drive anywhere. They're afraid to go to work. They have become, once again, invisible.

How does one go from invisible to visible?

It's not easy.

The Dreamers—the brave young people who were brought

to the United States as undocumented children and have since become the new political leaders of the Latino community—taught us that the first thing you have to lose is your fear.

They showed us this in 2010 when four of them marched from Miami to Washington to draw attention to their struggle. Many of us feared that they would be arrested along the way and deported to countries they did not know. But that's not what happened.

Those same Dreamers who in 2012 were not allowed to set foot in the White House because of their undocumented status were the ones who finally convinced President Obama that he indeed had the legal authority to approve an executive action and make Deferred Action for Childhood Arrivals a reality.

Their strategy worked.

In June 2016, I was invited to Houston to a conference of United We Dream, the primary organization of Dreamers in the United States. The place was filled with rebellious passion. It was clear to me that the new leadership of the Latino community was there and not in Washington.

I took the opportunity to talk about the difference between their parents and them. I said that I was very afraid that their parents would become the "sacrificial generation." What did I mean by that? That they were part of a group that, despite decades of effort, was never able to legalize their migratory status. But still they stayed in the United States so that their children could legally live here and prosper. They made this sacrifice for their children.

And we're already witnessing the results. The Dreamers are as American as any of us. They just don't have the paperwork to prove it. That's how they feel, and they let everyone know it.

Many Dreamers are the first in their families to attend college. I'm always excited to meet Dreamers at the nation's top universities. They study in places that their parents never could have imagined.

But the contrast between the tactics wielded by the Dreamers and those employed by their parents could not be more stark. The older generation believed that the most important thing was not to make any waves. Keep quiet and don't draw any attention to yourself, period. That was the way to get ahead in life. And they were right.

Their tactics of silence produced results. Many of their children were born here in the United States—and were therefore U.S. citizens with all requisite rights—and thousands of those born outside the country have been protected under DACA.

After many conversations with the Dreamers and their parents, I began to notice a certain sense of impatience among the Dreamers. Why had their parents remained silent for so long? Why did they not speak up and protest? Why didn't they go out and fight for their rights?

There are no easy answers to these questions. Suffice it to say that those were different times. The parents of today's Dreamers learned to survive by staying silent, invisible, virtually immobile. And there, while nobody was watching, was where they worked and raised their families.

It served them. But not their children, who decided to change the rules of the game.

Their parents were invisible, so the Dreamers want to be as visible as possible.

Their parents learned to use silence to their advantage. Dreamers want to be heard.

Their parents waited patiently for politicians to acknowledge them. Dreamers forced candidates to address them and their agenda.

Their parents never would have dared to confront members of Congress or occupy their offices. Dreamers aren't afraid of doing exactly this.

Their parents waited patiently and prayed for the best. Dreamers demanded immigration reform for themselves and for their parents.

Two different eras with two very different sets of tactics.

I have learned a lot from the Dreamers, which is why I dedicated this book to them. While I was in Houston, I told them that when I faced off with Donald Trump at the press conference in Iowa, the first thing I asked myself was, What would the Dreamers do?

They remind me so much of Rosa Parks.

On December 1, 1955, when she refused to give up her seat on a bus to a white passenger in Montgomery, Alabama, she knew that the law was against her. But she did it anyway. There are times when civil disobedience is necessary. And her simple gesture of defiant freedom kicked off the civil rights movement here in the United States.

I believe that Dreamers are doing the same thing: rebelling against unjust laws. They stand at the forefront of a new civil rights movement in the United States, one in which nobody is illegal, regardless of the papers you may or may not carry in your wallet.

That's why I dream with them.

Latinos: The Struggle
to Define Ourselves

———

I t is getting ever more difficult to define ourselves.

We are so many different things.

Latinos are staging a true demographic revolution in the United States, but at the same time, another revolution is taking place within the Hispanic community. Something very interesting began happening around the turn of the century.

After two decades during which most of the growth in the Latino population depended on immigrants coming from Latin America, things began to change. With a birth rate slightly higher than the U.S. average, more than half of Hispanic population growth was being generated from inside America's borders. According to the Pew Research Center, from 2000 to 2010, 9.6 million Latinos were born in the

United States, compared with 6.5 million who arrived here as immigrants.

This will have enormous consequences.

First, this shows that many Latin Americans no longer believe the United States is as attractive as it may have been before. The dangers of traveling north, increased security at the border, and the stress of living under constant persecution has caused millions of Latin Americans to stay in their countries of origin. They might not earn what they could here, but little by little, economic conditions are improving, and they are able to live their lives without constantly looking over their shoulders for ICE agents.

Here in the United States, these new citizens do not have to hide in the shadows, as many of their parents did, and will eventually reach voting age. They will never forget the fear and anxiety their parents endured, and their political convictions will doubtless be defined by these experiences. No one should be surprised if, in a decade or two, there is a very active Hispanic electorate with a very long and detailed memory. When someone mistreats your mother or father, it's something that you'll never forget.

Even for those with Spanish-speaking Latin American parents, being born in the United States has a decisive influence. First and foremost, English becomes the essential language.

Spanish is spoken in most Hispanic families to varying degrees. It is the language of our emotions, and it maintains our connection to the generations that preceded us: the grandson with the grandfather, the *te quiero* before leaving the house, the words that accompany the embraces during every time of joy or pain. The United States is the only country I know where people seem to believe that speaking one language is better than speaking two or three. But even those who are fully bilingual are aware of the fact that, here, English is the language of power and communication.

By 2012, only 35 percent of U.S. Hispanics were born in another country. This means that at least two-thirds grew up with English as their primary language.

And then it was my turn to witness this change firsthand.

As I mentioned, I have been working at Univision since 1984. For decades, the company philosophy was to focus on Spanish. Some of the stricter executives did not want us to use any English words during our broadcasts. And the strategy worked to perfection. Univision has been the leading Spanish-language media corporation since it was first established in 1962 as Spanish International Network, or SIN, in San Antonio, Texas.

But early in the twenty-first century—right around the time of the 9/11 terrorist attacks—we began to notice a demographic change among Latinos in general and within our own homes in particular. Our children were no longer watching Spanish-language programming. Sometimes, of course, they would join us for a soccer game or some other important event, but when the parents turned on a telenovela or the news, the kids would go into another room and seek shelter on their computers or smartphones.

Univision and Spanish-language television have a guaranteed future. According to the Pew Research Center, three out of four Latinos still speak Spanish. The market continues to grow thanks to a well-earned reputation for standing up for the community and providing very different programming from what you might find on the English-language channels. We cover all of Latin America as if it were local news, and we don't just report the facts, we also understand journalism as a public service. Our audience expects us to be a guide when it comes to issues such as immigration, health, and how, in general, to operate in American society. We give a voice to those who have none, and we defend our audience's rights. The civic and social orientation of our role is not often found on similar English programs.

We also have an advantage over them. Millions of Spanish-speaking immigrants will continue to arrive in the United States over the next few decades and will quickly become part of our audience. But at the same time, we have to recognize that younger Latinos are choosing to inform themselves and communicate more in English. I see it in my own home.

That's why the Fusion channel was created in 2013. It was Univision's first foray into the English-language market, and it soon spread out into a number of digital sites. The original idea was to create a channel for younger, English-speaking Hispanics. But we soon realized that would have been a strategic mistake. Viewer studies indicated that they didn't want something geared strictly for Latinos, who felt wholly a part of the greater United States. With that in mind, Fusion was created for all millennials, not just Latinos.

The experiment is ongoing and the results continue to be the same: 69 percent of second-generation and 83 percent of third-generation Latinos watch the majority of their television in English, according to the Pew Research Center. Why? Because 63 percent and 80 percent of them, respectively, think in English.

A similar trend is taking place in the news media. More and more Latinos are choosing to get their news solely in English: 32 percent in 2012, up from 22 percent in 2006. And adult Hispanics who say they watch at least some news programs in English rose from 78 to 82 percent during that same period of time.

All of this is the natural result of a community that grows more from children being born in the United States than from adults arriving from south of the border. Thus, over the course of a couple of generations, English is becoming the dominant language. Even Latinos who prefer to speak primarily in Spanish are of the belief that English is necessary to be successful in this country.

Most interesting of all is that this rapid process of English becoming the dominant language does not necessarily mean that Latinos consider themselves "typical Americans."

In 2012, the Pew Research Center conducted a fascinating study titled *When Labels Don't Fit: Hispanics and Their Views of Identity*, which concluded that nearly half of all Hispanics—47 percent—don't consider themselves "typical Americans." And it should come as no surprise that people who speak primarily Spanish, who were born somewhere else, or who have lower levels of education or income might feel less American than others.

I don't feel like a "typical American" myself. Many of us don't. How could you if your parents are deported, if the police are profiling you, if you're the victim of racism, or if the president himself insults your family? How could you if you lack the same opportunities as others simply because of your last name, your accent, or your skin color?

There is nothing typical about that.

Which is why, when asked what we are, very few of us say "American." Just over half—51 percent—prefer to identify with the country of their family's origin: Mexican, Venezuelan, Cuban, Colombian, and so on. One in four (24 percent) choose "Latino" or "Hispanic," while only one in five (21 percent) describe themselves as "American."

This is not to insult the United States or to imply some lack of loyalty. It simply reflects the dynamic complexity of our intermixed and intermingled families. We come from various countries, we have different types of immigration statuses, we incorporate a multitude of races and religions, and we share a very unequal command of languages.

But at the same time, there are some who do feel like "typical Americans" and who do not make any particular distinction between themselves and the rest of the U.S. population. *The New York Times* has referred to them as the "post-Hispanic Hispanics." They do not speak Spanish as their primary language, and they identify more with the ideas of their political party or social group than with their ethnicity.

Despite all that, integration into a group can never truly be complete. As Professor Roberto Suro wrote in *Strangers Among Us*, "Latinos are not on a straight track to becoming whites, but they are not indelibly marked as nonwhite outsiders, either." Suro describes perfectly how difficult it is to assign a permanent identity to Latinos, owing to their tremendous social, geographic, and linguistic mobility. Latinos can visit for a few months or stay for the rest of their lives; they can speak English, Spanish, or Spanglish at home; they can feel like foreigners living in a foreign country; or they can feel completely at home and identify themselves as fully American.

Latinos run the gamut from the fully integrated post-Hispanic Hispanics to those who are marginalized in the extreme, like many newly arrived undocumented immigrants.

The clearest official effort to unite us began with the 1980 census, which used the word "Hispanic" for the first time. In the 2000 census, the word "Latino" was added. But in fact, we can be many things at once: we can identify ourselves as black, white, or indigenous; we can associate ourselves with the country of our father, our mother, or neither; we can emphasize the city of our birth or the nation whose passport we carry; we can say we speak with or without an accent; we can belong to the largest or the smallest of groups; or we can reinvent ourselves based on a tiny characteristic hidden inside every family.

There is a lot of biology and geography in our sense of identity, but also a lot of will. We are what we were born as, but also what we want to be.

In very general terms, we are part of a group with origins in Latin America and Spain and that now resides in the United States. That's it: that's the most basic generalization we can make. But the combinations are almost endless.

I am a Mexican who lives in the United States and an American who was born and raised in Mexico. I have two passports; I vote in two countries; I am an immigrant with two American children. I am bilingual; I speak Spanish with a Mexico City accent, and I speak English with a newcomer's accent. And I insist on being all things at once. No one can force me to choose.

The author Isabel Allende feels the same way. She once told me about the frustration she experiences when journalists ask her to choose between Chile and the United States. Even after the terrorist attacks of September 11, 2001, she understood that she did not have to choose. That day she felt very American, very supportive of her neighbors in San Francisco, very close to her compatriots in New York.

It's the same for me. For clarity and simplicity, I would like to be able to say that I am Mexican or American or whatever else and have that be it. But I would be lying. I'm from right here and I'm from out there. And I'm not at war with myself about it. I've learned to manage the diversity within myself and to leap over boundaries at will, both physically and emotionally.

It wasn't always like this. It took me twenty-five years to become a U.S. citizen. I could have done it much earlier, but I waited. My rationale was that once I had spent the same number of years in the United States as I had in Mexico, I would finally become a citizen. And so it was.

But there was something else to it. I had been covering the wars in Afghanistan and Iraq, and I was well aware of how a president could make decisions regarding the lives of the thousands of U.S. citizens and legal immigrants serving in the armed forces. And I wanted to make sure that whoever was occupying the White House was someone who could be trusted with such a personal decision. But the only way to do that was to vote, and for that I needed to become a citizen.

In 2003, I was deeply disappointed with President George W. Bush's decision to invent weapons of mass destruction in order to justify a brutal war in Iraq. Yes, Saddam Hussein was a dictator, but he had no such weapons, and he had nothing to do with the terrorist attacks of 9/11.

I promised myself that I would vote in the 2008 elections. I would turn fifty that year, having spent twenty-five of those years in Mexico and twenty-five in the United States.

Mexico is a wondrous and beautiful country, filled with supportive and caring people. It's a place where you will never feel alone. And the United States is an extremely generous nation that gave me freedoms and opportunities I could never have found anywhere else in the world.

At one point I thought it was going to be difficult for me to participate in the swearing-in ceremony. After all, this was a process twenty-five years in the making. But as soon as I understood that I wouldn't have to give up my past, my origins, or my traditions, I was able to accept everything with serenity and a sense of inner peace.

I wasn't subtracting anything. I was adding.

Something truly beautiful occurs when you embrace a new nation and that nation embraces you back. It has to be reciprocal in order for it to work. The country adopts you, but you also have to adopt it.

Part of my job is to take a critical and independent look at what isn't working or what's harming any given nation on earth. It can be difficult to understand, but often it's a true labor of love when you do what you can to improve the place where you live. You critique the things that really matter to you, the things that you love about it. It's not a betrayal or a lack of solidarity.

It's my job, and it's my country.

Being an Immigrant
in the Trump Era

———

My accent betrays me.

I say just a few words in English, and people already know that I wasn't born in the United States. That I'm from somewhere else. I've been learning English for over three decades, and I don't think I'll ever be able to speak it perfectly. I can communicate easily enough with most Americans, but my accent is ever present.

Many recognize it as a Mexican accent, but few know that there's more to it than just that. It's a *chilango* accent, from the northern part of Mexico City, where there's a bit of a lilt to the words. That will always be there.

Many people don't like it when I speak English with an accent. Especially when I do so on television, which is evidenced by the comments I get on social media. And this reminds me of a great interview that radio journalist Terry Gross did with the South African comedian Trevor Noah when his book, *Born a Crime*, was published. Noah, who replaced Jon Stewart after he stepped down from *The Daily Show*, speaks six languages and is an expert at identifying and copying accents.

"When you hear somebody speaking in an accent, it's almost like they're invading your language," Noah said during the interview on *Fresh Air*. "It feels like an invasion of something that belongs to you. And, immediately, we change."

It's an acute observation. The fact of the matter is that a language such as English does not belong to anyone and we can speak it as we please to the best of our ability. But inevitably, someone will feel uncomfortable or even threatened by your accent, and that can make you feel very out of place.

Being an immigrant is inherently tied to this feeling. Occasionally for an entire lifetime. This much is clear in Edward Said's book *Out of Place*.

Said was a scholar born in Palestine during the time of British rule. He studied in the United Kingdom and had taught at several universities in the United States. In his book, he explains what it's like to come from many different worlds and feel many different streams coursing inside of you: "I occasionally experience myself as a cluster of flowing currents. I prefer this to the idea of a solid self, the identity to which so many attach so much significance. These currents, like the themes of one's life, flow along during the waking hours, and at their best, they require no reconciling, no harmonizing. . . . A form of freedom, I'd like to think, even if I am far from being totally convinced that it is. . . . With so many dissonances in my life I have learned actually to prefer being not quite right and out of place."

I find it interesting that Said describes this sense of being out of place as "a form of freedom." In a way, it is. Many immigrants experience a moment of clarity during which they feel powerful and free. The reasoning goes more or less like this: If I can manage to leave my country of origin and succeed in a new one, there's nothing on earth that can stop me. We are literally from many places.

The immigrant—the stranger—can choose to have many lives and can even choose to return, or try to return, to the one left behind. All of these different possibilities (or currents, as Said would say) of life exist within us simultaneously. Occasionally, one will impose itself on another, but none of them ever truly disappear.

This fluid sense of identity is precisely what bothers many people. They would rather Latinos be easily defined and have their loyalties lie solely with the country in which they live. But their historical reality—let alone their daily lives—is quite different from that of most Americans. We live (and some are even born) with two mother tongues, not just one. There are days where I begin in Spanish, read *The New York Times* in English, talk to my mother in Mexico, write my column in Spanish, check its translation into English, speak with my children in Spanglish, give an interview with CNN or Fox News, host *Noticiero Univision* in Spanish, drive home listening to MSNBC or a Beatles station on the radio, log on to Facebook and Twitter in both languages, and finally go to sleep, where I have fully bilingual dreams. Such a life—such a journey, really, with a history shared between north and south and between two languages—could never be a "typically American" one. I'm sorry, but it's just not possible.

There are days where I speak almost entirely in English, eat salads and hamburgers, and feel completely attached to the United States. There are other days, such as when the Mexican national soccer team is playing, that I can't help shouting out in Spanish and bask in the sense of belonging with other Mexicans.

And there are days when I am alone, very alone indeed.

I've never felt it more than one New Year's Eve in Los Angeles. I hadn't gone back to Mexico because of work and instead had been invited to a party downtown. When the clock struck midnight, everyone around me embraced and wished one another a happy New Year. But I didn't have anyone there. That's when I realized I was totally by myself.

I was an immigrant.

Alone.

However much you may have integrated yourself into your adoptive country, you will inevitably feel out of place from time to time. You will feel a physical and mental sense of displacement (which I actually prefer to the Spanish word, *desplazamiento*), and no matter how much you wish it were otherwise, you will know that you don't belong.

Of course, this isn't always the case. A friend once told me that my daughter, Paola, who had just been born, would end up saving me. And she was right. Paola made me understand what was truly important in life, and because of that, I held on to the United States. A few years later, the birth of my son, Nicolás, helped me reconfirm my decision to remain here in this country. Plus, he became my best English teacher.

How can people live far away from their children? I don't think I could have done it. A parent's first obligation is to be present, to literally be there for their children. My children's lives were in the United States, so mine would be, too.

Nothing ties you closer to a country than having your children born there. It will transform both your plans and your way of life. All of a sudden, the thoughts you harbored of one day returning to your country of origin are gone, and you realize that you will never permanently leave the United States. Throughout history we have seen how immigrants gradually pay less and less attention to what's going on in their countries of origin, how they send less and less money back to their extended family members, and how, after two or three generations, their children or grandchildren have almost lost the emotional or psychological connection with the nation of their parents and grandparents.

This process of integration took place in an almost organic way from the mid-1960s through the end of the twentieth century. But after the terrorist attacks of September 11, 2001, anti-immigrant sentiment—including state and local laws that made life all but impossible for some foreigners—gradually grew, leading to the emergence of Donald Trump's presidential candidacy. This has all but shattered the centuries-long tradition of accepting immigrants into American society.

Of course, this wasn't the first time that groups of immigrants have been rejected en masse. The suffering once endured by the Irish, Chinese, and Japanese is now being felt by Latinos and Muslims and possibly will be by Asians in a few more decades. What's different about this particular occasion is the extent and intensity of the attacks on foreigners . . . and the fact that some of the attacks are coming from the president of the United States himself.

Something like this has never occurred before.

Trump's original plan during the campaign for massive deportations was brutal and unprecedented in the history of this country. In August 2015, he told NBC journalist Chuck Todd that the eleven million undocumented immigrants living in the United States would either have to leave the country or be deported. "They have to go," he said during an interview on a private plane. "They have to go. Chuck, we either have a country, or we don't have a country."

And according to CBS, in September of that same year, during a conference call with members of the Republican Party, Trump set dates for his massive wave of deportations: "I think it's a process that can take eighteen months to two years if properly handled," he said. "I will get them out so fast that your head would spin, long before I even can start the wall. They will be out of here."

Let's do the math, horrifying as it is.

To deport eleven million people over the course of two years, you would need an army or some other similarly sized force. This would be a much larger event than Operation Wetback, which removed over one million Mexicans back in 1954.

Trump's aggressive plan would require identifying, detaining, and deporting more than fifteen thousand people per day. Getting them out of the country would require at least thirty Boeing 747s per day. In the meantime, housing them would require the use of stadiums and other public spaces. The daily images of families being torn apart and destroyed would be leading newscasts across the globe.

Further, what about the 4.5 million American children who have at least one undocumented parent? Would they be deported along with their mothers or fathers, or would they be left to the care of the state?

What Trump proposed was terror and intolerance.

And with this plan, he was elected president of the United States.

For me, it's personal.

How could we not feel attacked and rejected when over half of Latinos eighteen years of age and older are foreign born? How do you remain calm when your country's elected leader is planning to deport your neighbors, your coworkers, your relatives? Those who feed and care for you? How can he dare ask for the Latino vote with a straight face while at the same time telling the Hispanic population that he wants to deport their parents and siblings?

How do you not feel like a second-class citizen when the entire history of the United States is filled with examples of immigrants eventually becoming citizens, yet now there is not even a means of legalizing the undocumented, leaving them without a path to citizenship?

Part of the American experience is having an immigrant past—legal or otherwise—and then participating in a civic process that grants you the same rights as everyone else.

There is nothing more American than incorporating and integrating those who come from outside the nation's borders, regardless of their accents or origins.

But that experience of belonging is beginning to crack.

The experiment known as the United States is based on the extraordinary process of converting "others" into "us." And for the first time in our nation's history, this process has been halted via a presidential initiative that offers little hope for the future.

Trump and his supporters refuse to accept those they consider "criminals" or "invaders." But these "invaders" about whom Trump complains are the same ones who clean and maintain his hotels and restaurants, and they would never be invited to join him at the table.

I am convinced that this effort to push us aside will fail. But it will take years and perhaps even decades to overcome. In the end, the demographic revolution that the United States is currently experiencing—in which minorities will become the new majority—will end up overwhelming xenophobia, rejecting the radical extremist groups, and the United States can continue with its tradition of ethnic diversity, multiculturalism, and acceptance of immigrants.

Despite my optimism for the long term, we must acknowledge that we are living in a very dark and dangerous time in U.S. history. It is truly disheartening to see that ideas, proposals, and laws are arising systematically in the White House and both chambers of Congress designed to attack immigrants and minorities without justification.

This is the hand the United States has dealt us, and we have to play it in order to change direction.

What does it mean to be a Latino immigrant in the United States during the Trump era? First of all, it means being a member of a persecuted and discriminated minority. But it is a growing minority that now knows, for the very first time, what it means to hold a certain amount of power.

Being a minority does have at least one advantage: sooner or later, everything becomes greater. And this is why we must maintain an attitude of revolution, of constant struggle, especially if your particular group is being misunderstood or marginalized. How could you not fight back when you're being insulted, when your neighbors are being deported, when you realize that others have more opportunities than you, when you are marginalized for the way you talk or because of the color of your skin? How could you not, when you are made to feel that this is not your country?

One of the things I have most admired about the United States is the inherent conviction that things will always get better, that people will overcome obstacles, and that there will be opportunities for all. It is a philosophy for life that has been built up for more than two centuries. Or better yet, it is a matter of faith (which, incidentally, has nothing to do with religion).

There are nations whose history lends a sense of pessimism and skepticism. The United States is not one of them. Even during the most trying of times, such as these, there is always a case for optimism, a clear spirit of improvement, and the certainty that everything can be changed.

Despite the bad news and negative atmosphere, this is the country where my children were born, and I believe much more in them—and in the power of their generation—than I do in the racist, xenophobic, and destructive ideas of Donald Trump.

So here I'm going to bet on my children and the country they want to build for themselves.

When I Return to Mexico

—

Though I travel to Mexico several times a year for both personal and professional reasons, I have to keep in mind that I have lost touch with the country to the extent that it can be reduced to a series of news reports, snapshots, and outbursts that are not always tied directly to reality. Sometimes I think of Mexico with a true sense of nostalgia. On other occasions, I fall into the trap of stereotyping it as a nation of extreme violence and hidden graves. And then there are the times where I can imagine it as an almost magical place, as if I were a foreigner watching it for the first time.

I have written many columns on Mexico, most of which have to do with politics and the transition to democracy, which is as difficult as it is incomplete. Here, I would like to share three short essays that I have selected and updated because they reflect, in the following order, my nostalgia, my frustration, and my astonishment with Mexico.

"GOING HOME"
(From December 2015)

We're stuck. It's almost midnight, and Mexico City's airport doesn't have enough gates to accommodate all the flights that are landing.

So we wait: a half hour in an airliner at a standstill, then another half hour in a small bus, then an hour in line at customs. By daybreak, there is a chill in the air. But it doesn't matter. I'm finally home, for a little while—to see my mother, my siblings, and the city I left almost thirty-three years ago.

Those of us who can go home to Mexico from the United States do so at least once a year, preferably around Christmastime or for New Year's. This year in particular, world events have made all of us more conscious of just where home is.

Whenever I visit Mexico City, familiar flavors and aromas are the first things that spark my nostalgia. I binge on tacos, Mexican-style eggs, shrimp broth, Churrumais snacks, Maria Cookies with La Abuelita butter, glasses of cold milk mixed with Pancho Pantera Choco Milk powder. These were all my favorites growing up. Today, they are comfort foods for those of us who return to visit—and they always bring back a Mexico that exists only in my memory.

The conversations with my family are full of

reminiscences—"what happened to what's-his-name" and so on. Our talk eventually turns to who might now be living in "our house."

One of my siblings pulls up a photo on his phone. It's of our old house in Bosques de Echegaray, in the state of Mexico, where we grew up. Our parents sold the house many years ago, and it's now painted yellow. I notice that the old tree at the entrance has been removed. It's still our house, the one that my soul—whatever that is—acknowledges as my home.

Now my life is anchored in Miami, my second home—a generous, multicultural city that is populated mostly by people who were born elsewhere. As a good friend often points out, Hispanics in Miami are treated as first-class citizens. He's right. Nobody is an "alien" in Miami.

But many Mexicans, documented or not, who are living in other parts of the United States—in Chicago, in Houston, in Los Angeles, in New York—are simply exhausted. They scrape by for years, doing jobs that Americans won't, yet they remain far from achieving the American Dream—a nice house, a decent job, good schools for their children, and the promise that things will be better tomorrow.

Meanwhile, Donald Trump, who is running for the Republican nomination for president, seems intent on making the lives of all immigrants miserable, and his messages of hatred and fear have only increased his popularity. And his anti-immigrant rhetoric is repeated constantly on social media.

For the first time since the "Operation Wetback"

program of 1954, more Mexicans are leaving the United States than entering. According to research from Pew, from 2009 to 2014, 1 million Mexicans returned to Mexico, while 870,000 came to the United States. This means that there are about 130,000 fewer Mexicans living here than there were a few years ago.

Yet Trump likes to talk about a Mexican invasion, even though he is very mistaken. Of course, it won't matter to him—Trump will continue to use fear as a strategy to win votes.

Many immigrants are returning to Mexico for good, despite the drug-related violence and public corruption that plague the nation and the failure of leadership from a president who prefers to hide from his problems. The lack of economic opportunities in the United States, coupled with an anti-immigrant sentiment, is becoming too much to bear.

At the end of my recent visit to Mexico, I boarded another plane and again felt torn. Yes, I was leaving loved ones behind in Mexico, but others were waiting for me in Miami. Home for me is not one but several places. That's what it means to be an immigrant.

The celebrated author Isabel Allende once pointed out to me that immigrants don't have to pick between one country and another.

They can belong to both.

"DAYS OF THE DEAD"
(From March 2017)

Authorities called it "the swimming pool" because the bodies in this mass grave were buried so close together—more than 250 skulls were found. This is one of more than 120 unmarked graves unearthed since August of last year over a large area in Santa Fe, a town in the Mexican state of Veracruz.

But Mexico's president, Enrique Peña Nieto, and his administration have acted as if this gruesome discovery has nothing to do with them—as if this mass grave is located in some faraway country.

Last year the first bodies were found with the help of the Colectivo Solecito, or the "Little Sun Collective" in English—a group of 150 mothers who refuse to give up looking for their loved ones.

"We haven't heard of any declaration by President Peña Nieto," Lucía de los Ángeles Díaz, the founder of the Colectivo Solecito, told me recently. "The authorities charged with acknowledging the severity of the problem have failed to act."

Along with the administration's silence has come no funding to help identify the remains.

In Mexico, it seems that every day is Day of the Dead.

Last year, a person unknown to Lucía handed her a map labeled with crosses. Following a hunch, she took the map up a hill near Santa Fe, where she came across some of the hidden graves.

Lucía hasn't seen her son, Luis Guillermo, in almost

four years. Luis, nicknamed "DJ Patas," used to perform at the best parties in Veracruz. On June 28, 2013, as Luis was leaving an event in the early morning hours, armed men kidnapped him, Lucía says.

At first she had hoped it was an "express kidnapping"— where a victim is forced to withdraw money from several ATMs but is left alive to later share the frightening tale. Sadly, it wasn't that kind of kidnapping.

Lucía refuses to believe that her son might be in one of those pits in Veracruz. Even though she has found no clues to his whereabouts, she reminded me about several cases of missing persons in Mexico who were found years later.

She didn't cry during our discussion—for Lucía, this isn't the time to cry. "We don't question what we're doing," she told me. "We do it because we're mothers. We fight, and keep looking until we find them."

For tens of thousands of families in Mexico, the tragedy is redoubled: they can count on the authorities neither to find the lost ones nor to bring to justice the people who are responsible.

"It's very unfortunate to have a government that doesn't represent us, to have a government that isn't accountable," Lucía says, dressed in impeccable white, with a picture of her son on her lapel.

Mexico is a nation of graves. Peña Nieto's administration has overseen one of the most violent periods in the country's modern history. Since he took office in December 2012, more than 77,000 Mexicans have been killed, and more than 5,500 Mexicans have been kidnapped, according to official data.

Such staggering numbers seem to have numbed the Mexican people. As the shocking details about the grave in Veracruz started to trickle out this month, I expected to see mass protests on the streets of Mexico. I thought that the Mexican Congress would surely launch an independent investigation and that the president would go on national television to announce his plans to identify the bodies and punish the culprits. But none of that has happened.

Perhaps it's understandable. Two and a half years ago, forty-three students from Ayotzinapa went missing. To this day nobody knows where they are or what happened to them. What can we expect, then, for Lucía's son? In what sort of country does the discovery of 253 bodies in a pit not warrant action by the government? Such an atrocity can't simply be accepted.

"It would seem we live in the worst of all worlds," Peña Nieto said recently, "but we really don't."

Don't we? Ask Lucía and the other mothers from the Colectivo Solecito.

"THE LAST SUPPER"
(From July 2017)

Tulum, Quintana Roo, Mexico—I've never had a meal like this and may never taste its equal again. It was, simply put, a one-of-a-kind experience that may be impossible to repeat. So let me share it with you the only way I can: through words.

The celebrated chef René Redzepi, from Copenhagen's Noma—a restaurant that leading food critics consider one of the world's best—came to Tulum this spring and opened a pop-up restaurant for seven weeks. (Previously Redzepi had opened pop-ups in Sydney and Tokyo.) Last December, he offered seven thousand reservations to Noma Mexico at $600 each. All of them were snatched up within two hours.

The stakes were as high as the price tag.

Redzepi had to transform a parking lot in Tulum's tourist zone into a laboratory of gastronomic experimentation. Understandably, he didn't come to Mexico alone—he brought along his family and about one hundred employees from Noma in Copenhagen.

Redzepi and his assistants spent months exploring the traditional dishes and ingredients of the Yucatán Peninsula. They built an open kitchen and set up an outdoor dining room on the sand, under the palm trees. Then they launched a culinary revolution.

This whole experiment was about reimagining Mexican cuisine—tasting Mexico in a whole new way. What sort of experience could a renowned foreign chef create while using the local ingredients available to Mexicans?

The result was truly an epiphany. Redzepi and his team tasted the same food I grew up with in Mexico, but they saw it with a fresh perspective. They deconstructed it, rethought it, and reassembled it precisely.

In the process they introduced us to new sensations. For instance, Redzepi served a lot of flowers, in soup and as an entrée. Before that meal, I had only seen those flowers used as décor. After that first course, I gobbled up a *salbute* (or puffed tortilla) with grasshoppers, and a seaweed dish infused with *michelada* (a beer-based cocktail). I tried a ceviche prepared with broiled, marinated bananas. I had never tasted a softer octopus than Redzepi's *dzikilpak*, cooked for hours in maize dough inside a clay vase.

When a dish featuring *escamoles*, or ant eggs, arrived, my five dinner companions were a little intimidated. But the dish, whose history stretches back to Mexico's pre-Columbian times, was a delight—served on a tostada and surrounded by miniature local greens.

I ate young coconut with a pulp as soft as jelly, transformed into a tropical-Nordic hybrid with a garnish of Scandinavian caviar that Redzepi brought to Mexico.

A black mole sauce, traditionally served with chicken, was placed upon a baked *hoja santa*, a large-leafed Mexican herb. More recognizable were small tacos of "bald pig," a mix of crunchy and soft pork—a tribute to *cochinita pibil*, a slow-roasted pork dish. For dessert, we were served grilled avocado ice cream and chocolate with chile.

I'm no food critic, and after three surgeries on my nose, I have little sense of smell. But each of those delightful dishes had its own unique, complex story that could be experienced by all the senses.

We diners could hear enthusiastic cheers from the kitchen every time a dish was served. Four Yucatecan women were making tortillas by hand. The restaurant's young servers, aware that they were part of something special, were meticulous in their description of the dishes—a sign that they loved the food.

Asked why he liked working with Redzepi, one server said: "Because he forces us to strive for excellence."

I happened to be there for the last supper—the night

that Noma was closing its doors in Tulum. Once the final dessert was brought out of the kitchen, toasts and laughter followed. "We did it," said Redzepi.

In the end, Mexico demonstrated that it was the best country in the world for this great experiment. With the same foods available to everyone, these foreigners were able to create something entirely different. When they speak about Mexico, they aren't thinking of mass graves, election rigging, spying, or corruption. No, they think of endless possibilities and resources—a joyful, almost magical place with solidarity and "the prettiest service in the world," as an American hotelier put it.

I wish every Mexican could see their country with the same optimism, respect, and hope with which Redzepi and his associates did. When the meal was over, I hugged the chef and told him: "Thanks for letting me see my country in a different way."

A Mexican Childhood

———

There is a particular photograph that makes me very uneasy: one of my dad carrying me in his arms. I would have been just a few months old. He looks very serious, almost distant, as if I weren't really there. I'm dressed all in blue, probably wool, with my mouth open and a little wave of blond hair parting my head in half. It might just be the first picture ever taken of me. But it's also the only picture I have of my dad and me.

The only one.

I've been looking through my albums and on my computer for other pictures, and I just can't find any. There are some of the whole family together, but none of just my dad and me.

My relationship with my dad wasn't an easy one. It didn't flow naturally. It seemed to get caught up in the individual moments. I can only remember playing with him once: he tried to kick a soccer ball, and I tried to make him believe that everything was going great. But in fact he struck the ball poorly, with the toe of his shoe instead of the instep, and the attempt at some father-son bonding ended after only a few seconds. There must have been other occasions where we played together, but I can't remember them.

It is true, though, that he taught me how to play chess, which is a game I still enjoy to this very day. But our matches were never simply games: they were scenes of confrontation between father and son. He always beat me, except for one occasion when I caught him in checkmate after a careless move on his part. Never again did he make that mistake.

He once took my siblings and me to a bounce house, but mostly he liked to bring pastries with him when he came home from work, especially *rayaditos*, which are a kind of Mexican madeleine.

I didn't see much of him from Monday to Friday, and on the weekends I mostly saw the back of his head as he drove us to visit my grandparents. Maybe his own father hadn't played much with him, and he'd never thought to alter that behavior.

We didn't talk often. The sex conversation took place during a quick drive from the house to the mall. What he said amounted to "Let me know if you need help." Of course, I didn't let him know about anything.

My dad had a strict set of rules for the household. When will you be home? Don't leave without some money in your pocket. Call if you're running late. Do your homework. When I was younger, I was afraid of him. If I saw him reading the newspaper in the living room, I would go somewhere else.

Every once in a while he would scream and shout, but as I grew older I came to understand that that's just how he was, that the shouting was harmless, that he was never going to change, and that setting up rules was just his way of loving and protecting us.

In his mind, there were only four legitimate professions: an architect (like him), an engineer, a lawyer, or a doctor. None of these interested me. When I informed him that I was going to major in communications, his response was simply, "Well, what are you going to do with that?"

It was a fairly disparaging reaction to my career choice. I have to admit that there was a joyful bit of rebellious intent behind making a decision that upset my dad. If he didn't approve, then it must be a good idea. Now, of course, I understand that his only concern was for my own financial welfare, so that I wouldn't have to struggle through life the way he did when he was younger.

So in spite of my dad's protests, I studied the subjects that I enjoyed the most. He hadn't, and it showed. Ramos the architect was also a great magician, and he loved performing tricks for us. I always thought it might have been his true vocation in life, but my grandfather forced him into something he didn't enjoy.

Despite everything to the contrary, this story has a happy ending.

After I moved to the United States, I was able to make peace with my dad. The tension and detachment that we felt when we were younger had blossomed into a warm and loving relationship. When I left, I broke the precast mold of what, for him, the father-son relationship should be like. Once he was able to free himself from this obligation, he began to see me through a new set of eyes . . . as I was able to do with him.

We were finally able to embrace. Whenever I went back to Mexico, we would spend some time together. Sometimes it was in silence, as the Ramos family is wont to do, but we enjoyed and appreciated it a lot. And I would always say goodbye with a hug and a kiss that I knew was for both of us.

Television sealed the deal. From his apartment in Mexico City, he could watch me deliver the news in Miami. Afterward, I would call him on the phone to see what he thought about it all. "I didn't pay much attention to the news," he would say. "I just wanted to see you."

He usually commented on the ties I wore. He loved wearing boldly designed ties himself, and knowing that, I would try to wear something that he would enjoy. And when I would hear him mention my *corbatita*—my little tie—over the phone, I knew that I had succeeded.

One of the greatest tragedies any immigrant can experience is not being with your loved ones when they die. I knew that my father was ill—he had been through a couple of heart attacks—but I never expected my mother to call me one night with the news that things had become quite serious. The next call was to let me know that he had passed away.

I was in the newsroom, about to give the nightly broadcast, and—in a state of total denial—I went through with it. Fortunately my colleagues were with me, and they sent me home to Mexico City the next morning so I could attend the funeral.

Who would have thought it? Television—the career my father never would have wanted for me—was what ended up bringing us together in the end.

But I grew up rebelling against him.

And against the abusive Catholic priests who ran my elementary school and high school.

And against the prevailing antidemocratic system in Mexico.

So when faced with an authoritarian father, authoritarian teachers, and an authoritarian country, I had no choice but to become a journalist.

Immigrants don't remember abstractions. In my case, I don't formulate a generic image of Mexico like you might find in a library book. No. I think very concrete things: specific moments that, over time, have surely been transformed into memories that are very different from the events that actually happened.

I remember spending the day in the street playing soccer with my brothers, Alejandro, Eduardo, and Gerardo. We were only about a year apart from one another. We shared clothes and two carpeted rooms, and we grew together like a band, which was perfect when picking teams. We played in the street, forming the goal with two large stones that we had to move aside whenever a car wanted to pass. We played with our neighbors, making up Olympic and World Cup championships and all sorts of other competitions, whether it was on foot or on a bicycle. My knees were perpetually covered in scabs. When we got bored with running around, we would go to houses still under construction and set up in our fort—something of a bat cave—until the masons showed up and ran us off. My sister, Lourdes, discovered the fort one day after having

returned home from a long trip to Canada. She was the youngest of the family and spent her time with her friends playing
at home with their dolls while my brothers and I were hanging out in the street. Much, much later we would become very
close friends and confidants.

Every morning we would hop on a bus that would take us to
the school located on the outskirts of the city. But sometimes
for me it seemed as if they were ferrying us off to hell. It was
a Catholic school run by Benedictine priests, who were, in
my childish mind, the closest thing to the devil incarnate.
Padre William, Padre Rafael, and Padre Hildebrando pulled
us by the hair and beat us on the hands and buttocks with
their shoes, but by far their most sadistic form of punishment was to make the student/victim stand in the middle of
the patio with his arms extended in the form of a cross while
holding stacks of books in his hands. I remember that physical and psychological abuse being quite frequent. To them,
it was a matter of discipline; for us, it was a matter of fear.
One day, Padre Hildebrando was upset about some trouble
we were causing and said, "The storm is coming, so you'd
better get on your knees and pray." Mockingly, we got on
our knees. The punishment lasted for several days, and they
forced us to confess each and every Friday. But the priests to
whom we were confessing our sins were the same ones who
were responsible for imposing discipline at the school. So of
course, we all learned to lie. I was terrified of the story of hell.
They told us that if we died without confessing, we would
be condemned to spend all eternity with the devil himself.

Around that same time I went to see the movie *The Exorcist*, which proved to be a grave mistake. The terrible images haunted me for years, whether I was awake or asleep in my dreams. That was supposedly why we had to confess? Creating something of a bank account with heaven, I would make up sins to confess on Fridays, on the off chance that I would commit a sin the next week and die before I had a chance to confess again. To me, Padre William was the most menacing of the three. His eyes always seemed to be filled with hatred, and the little acts of torture to which he subjected us seemed to give him some sense of pleasure. To my young, frightened (terrified, really) eyes, he was a sadistic priest. He carried a neolite shoe sole—the kind he used to beat us with—in his back pocket as a constant warning. Once, I told him that I had to leave school early for some athletic training. My goal was to compete in the Olympics one day. His response was "You're no Superman." Maybe not, but I wasn't dumb, either. I suffered through this ordeal for ten years until one day I told my parents I couldn't take it anymore and I left. I did this the year before I was supposed to finish. I didn't want to give them the pleasure of graduating from their high school. I was no longer worried about going to hell: I was already there, and I had to get out. For all these reasons, it should come as no surprise that I ended up leaving the church and becoming suspicious of all organized religion. I was baptized as a Catholic, I took my First Communion, and I was forced to attend Mass on Sundays. But as soon as I was old enough to live on my own, I stopped going. Without even realizing it, I became an agnostic. I do not believe in divine justice, or that someone up in heaven determines what we do, or that things happen for a reason. People forge their own destiny, period. Padres Rafael, William, and Hildebrando were the least godly men I have ever known. The world is a very unfair place. As a journalist, I have seen some horrible things. If God exists, why would He allow this? We must be good people even if we are not assured of a prize in the end. I would love to have faith. It would be a great source of tranquility, particularly in my later years. But I simply do not. I do not know what will happen when I die. Nothing would make me happier than to be again with the ones I love the most. And if, in the end, I am wrong—if God indeed exists and there is a heaven where everyone can be happy for all eternity—well, I hope you will forgive me and still invite me to the party.

Recess at that school took place in the jungle. Once you set foot outside the classroom, you had to protect yourself from the bullies, who back then were more of a school-yard mafia who sparked terror in the hearts of the bravest among us. My main concerns were the Peñafiel brothers and El Caballo, the Horse. One day, one of the Peñafiel brothers punched my brother Alejandro during a basketball game, and, terrified, I warned him not to do it again. I was expecting him to beat me up, but apparently he decided to take it easy on me and never did it again. El Caballo was a different sort of bully. He was much bigger than the rest of us at that age, and he laughed when he punched someone in the head or shoved someone out of line so they would get in trouble with the teachers. When facing El Caballo, I had no choice but to align myself with El Perro, the Dog, which is what we called Armando, a tough but loyal friend who protected us from El Caballo's bullying. Lalo and Mario were my two best friends, and I mistakenly believed that they would be for life, because when you're a child, you often think that everything is for life. Teachers and priests all but disappeared during recess, so we had no choice but to defend ourselves as best we could. Virtually all the students had their break at the same time, and during a particularly rough patch, the older kids decided to play *calzón* on the playground. It was a brutal assault—I can't call it a game—in which a whole group of kids would rip off your underwear without having removed your pants. Of course, the weakest and smallest among us were the usual victims. I was spared, but to this day I still have painful memories of a classmate who never returned to school after suffering such painful and public humiliation. But that's how I learned to defend myself as a kid.

My mom turned out to be a rebel. The first rebel and the first feminist I ever met. The first one I ever loved. And it all started with chocolate. Ever since he was a kid, my dad enjoyed hot chocolate. But not just any hot chocolate: there was one special way that my grandmother Raquel would warm up the milk, add the perfect amount of cocoa, and then whip it just enough to get a little layer of foam rising above the rim of the cup. Before getting married, my mom learned how to make this most blessed of chocolate drinks, and she did so for many years until one day, after yet another embarrassing incident in which my father returned his cup because the foam hadn't risen to the proper height. After that, my mom decided she was done with making his hot chocolate. The rebellion had begun to brew. I now realize that an incident in Cuernavaca—where my mom suddenly got out of the car and refused to get back in while her husband and five children begged her to reconsider—was just a prelude. The war of independence in the Ramos household, which was indeed a feminist fight, was about to begin. With the money her grandfather had left her when he died, my mom bought a car of her own and shortly thereafter enrolled in college. Yes, it all happened in that order, and all because of my dad's damn cup of hot chocolate. My mom had a lot to rebel about. She was never allowed to go to high school. Instead, she attended a finishing school to learn how to become a wife and a homemaker. But she was never satisfied with that. Years later, when she saw her five children attending college, she decided she wanted to do the same for herself. She enrolled in some humanities courses at the Universidad Iberoamericana—the same university that my siblings and I all attended—and we often ran into each other in the hallways on campus. "I did what I wanted to do," she told me recently, her face a mixture of joy and determination. This was one of her great personal triumphs during a life that she dedicated to us, her children. Once, standing in the kitchen door, she started to tell me about happiness. I was just a kid and never had a talk with her like that, but she continued. Happiness is never permanent, she told me. It appears only at certain moments. And when it does, we must take advantage of it. And she knew what she was talking about. Her mother died of cancer the day she turned fifteen. She had been taken out of the room where her mother died, and no one bothered to tell her what had happened. They didn't even wake her up to attend the funeral. To this very day, my mother the rebel is still marked by moments such as these.

Once every year my dad would come home with a new car. There might not be money to repair the leak in the roof or pay for tuition, but there was enough for the latest model of his favorite car. Here's how the ritual took place: My father would pull up, honking the horn, and my siblings and I would run out from our rooms so that he could give us a ride around the block. If he was in the mood, he would take us out on the beltway, which we called "the rise" and which felt almost like a roller coaster. If we were lucky, the neighbors would be out and see Dad's new car, because we all wanted to show it off. My father hated distracting sounds. Anytime we dropped something on the floor, his head would whip around so he could register his displeasure with us. He preferred to crank up the music of his favorite orchestras on the car radio and would use one hand (sometimes even two!) to conduct his imaginary ensemble of musicians. The car also served as the confessional. My brothers and I all went there, in turn, to have the sex talk with our dad. A new car was the highest luxury to which the Ramos family could aspire. That, and one meal a year at a fine restaurant. I ordered shrimp every time. I loved them. But they were also the most expensive item on the menu. My dad was always the last to order. I always suspected that he waited in order to do a quick mental calculation of what the family had ordered, so that he could order something cheaper if necessary to make sure he had enough to pay for the meal.

Saturdays and Sundays were for soccer, *chicharrones*, and family. "Go say hello to your grandpa," my mom would say, and five pairs of tennis shoes would scurry up the stairs to surprise Abuelito Miguel standing in the bathroom or maybe even still in bed, reading one of his voluminous history books. He was my mom's dad, and he was a delight. He was born in 1900 and would often look back in amazement at how he grew up with so little. He would go on to witness the advent of electricity, trains, and airplanes. He was a generous man, grateful for life, and always in good spirits. When we went to his house, he would give the kids some *rompope*, a drink similar to eggnog, including alcohol, which made us feel very grown-up . . . and, I suppose, in rather high spirits. While the adults were enjoying their aperitifs in the living room, the kids would go upstairs to watch television, which was in black and white, of course, and often the reception was so bad that we had to stand next to the unit and act as an antenna in order to make out the picture. My grandpa would give us some *chicharrones* as a snack, and by dinnertime we were no longer hungry. He lived there with his sisters, Elsa, Martha, and Raquel Avalos. There were always people and music at Abuelito Miguel's house, and it was always fun to spend New Year's Eve there. The small yard was like a county fair: while we were playing soccer, my aunt Rocío was turning cartwheels, skirt and all, while the rest of the family was drinking tequila or Bloody Marys. Then we broke out the piñatas. The sudden sound of a stick breaking through the casing, and all that candy falling to the ground, is the closest thing there is to instant happiness. And we would dive for that candy more like piranhas than kids, devouring everything in our path. On the other hand, at the home of Abuelito Gilberto, my father's father, everything was serious and boring. After the children ate, they had to go outside so that the adults could eat in peace. After the meal, my grandfather would go upstairs to take his nap, and it was there in his room that we would go to say good night. He gave us candies—one apiece—along with *el domingo*, a few coins we could use to spend at the school store. When my grandfather Gilberto died, my grandmother Raquel Ramos inherited his money . . . or so I thought. In one of my many attempts to escape Mexico, I had been accepted into the London School of Economics and Political Science. It would be a great opportunity. So I went out to eat with her, and when it was time for dessert, I asked her for the $8,000 I would need in order to attend college in England for the year. I don't have the money, she said to me without even batting an eye. I wanted to tell her that Abuelito Gilberto would have helped me, and I wanted to ask her where all the money from the sale of his ranch had gone (he owned a ranch in the northern state of Coahuila, which I naively assumed also belonged to his children and grandchildren, though it never did). But it was all to no avail. That day, when she refused to give me the money to study abroad, I swore that finances would never again be an obstacle to achieving my dreams. I promised myself that this would never again happen to me or to those I love the most. And that's how it's been ever since. I wasn't able to study in London, but the events of that day changed my life and the lives of many other people.

———

I lived in a white, two-story house with what I believe was a red roof. You see, there are some things that I can no longer remember. It had a tall metal gate and a door that no one ever used. The garage was open and designed for two cars, though somehow we managed to park four. I slept in one of the upstairs rooms with Alejandro; Eduardo and Gerardo were in an adjoining room; and on the other side was my sister, Lourdes. The five of us shared a single bathroom. My parents slept in the larger room opposite mine, and next to them was the television room. It was there that I watched episodes of *Chabelo*, *Topo Gigio*, *The Munsters*, and—when I was allowed to stay up late—the series *Combat!*, which aired at ten o'clock. Downstairs was the living room (which we weren't allowed to enter, because it was "just for guests"), the kitchen, with a long metal grill for preparing the meals, a dining room, and a yard with grass and a handrail that we used as a goal while pretending to be Enrique Borja, the star striker for the Mexican national soccer team. There was no greater honor on earth than being called Borjita Ramos. He was a born goal scorer, and years later, when I had the privilege of getting to know him, he listened to me tell this ridiculous story from my youth without laughing right in front of me. The kitchen was like a hive. We went in to grab something from the refrigerator before running back out to play. It was there that I learned how to make butter-and-sugar sandwiches on white bread. I now realize that was my comfort food, and even today, when I'm feeling anxious or need something to take the edge off my hunger, I fix one for myself. And I usually pair it with a glass of cold chocolate milk, which is what my mother used to give me, "because children shouldn't drink coffee." To this day, I still don't drink coffee. The only danger was the pressure cooker my mom used to cook beans—which she cleaned one by one to make sure there were no pebbles among them—had the bad habit of exploding and leaving rather large splatters on the ceiling. And no, neither those stains nor the beans embedded in the walls were ever repaired by Ramos the architect. What he did do was request that a phone line be installed, a process that took years. Once the request was approved, we had to wait for the phone company to construct a few miles of landlines so that the phone could be physically connected to our house, which was located on the outskirts of Mexico City. Imagine a single phone line for seven people! There was no privacy whatsoever. There were three or four jacks spread throughout the house, and whenever the phone rang, everyone jumped to answer it. If someone was on a call, it was common to hear someone else pick up a receiver in another room to either listen in on the conversation or make strange noises so that the other person would be pressured into hanging up fast. I still remember the number, but I won't include it here because somehow it is still connected to the same house I grew up in, and I wouldn't want to bother the current tenants. There were never any parties in that house; birthdays and other important moments went uncelebrated. Recently I asked my mom why this was, and her reply was weighted with realism: "There was never any money, Jorgito." Exactly. Parties cost money, and when you have five children, the number of birthdays, holidays, and all other sorts of celebrations can start to add up. So the alternative was not to celebrate. Do nothing at all. Almost. The only party we ever hosted at home was when I graduated from college. My primary concern (other than getting a few bottles of wine) was that my friends not notice the huge leak right in the center of the living room ceiling, which Ramos the architect never saw fit to repair. The house itself was halfway down the street, and our next-door neighbors were the Sotres. They had four girls who were about the same ages as the four Ramos brothers. There were no romantic interests between us, but we spied on them through the windows, as I assume they did on us. The Aceves—Alejandro, Sergio, and Silvia—lived two houses down, and there was no greater weekend joy than to be invited over to swim in their backyard pool. It was the only thing like it on the block, and a real luxury. Sassa and Piff were almost right across the street from us; they spoke French with their mother (whom we affectionately called Oui Mama), and the school they attended let them grow their hair out long. Sassa was the first member of the group to start smoking cigarettes. The Hallivis lived across the intersection. Beto was the best-looking guy on the street, but it was his older brother, Luciano, who was the most popular because he was the first to get his own car. We would spend the afternoons sitting in his Volkswagen listening to cassette tapes. The Mier y Terán family almost never left their house, and the only thing we knew about them was that they went to some Opus Dei camps. I went once, and the only good thing about it was the freshly baked bread. I never went back again. The Prietos and the Montaño sisters completed the group. We popped in and out of all the houses on the block as if they were our own, and all the parents looked after us as if we were their own children.

Go ask your aunt Irma if she has any sugar, someone would say. *Where are your brothers? At Piff's house, racing toy cars. Well, we're getting ready to eat. I'm okay, I already had a sandwich at the Aceves' house.* There was an unspoken understanding among the inhabitants of the twenty-odd houses on that street that we were all part of a community. And that kind of magical protection extended well beyond the boundaries of the neighborhood. My mom used to send us to buy freshly made bread and tortillas at La Abeja, a bakery and shop that was a quick ten-minute walk from home. Nothing ever happened to us.

I learned the importance of sharing in that house. After all, you don't have much of a choice when you have a sister and three younger brothers. I learned you can always find a place to play, even if it's in the street. I learned to appreciate my friends and others close to me, because nobody chooses where to be born or where to grow up. I learned to be a rebel and a feminist from the excellent example set by my mother. I learned to improve as I grow, thanks to my father's genuinely caring and affectionate change in his behavior. I learned not to give up and to defend myself, whether it was from cruel priests in high school or the bullies on the playground. I learned to be self-sufficient and to not depend on anyone else. I learned not to expect anything from either my government or my grandmother. And I learned to rely not on the promises of heaven, but on personal dedication and the love and solidarity of others.

In other words, the most important things in life I learned in that house.

On Amphibians and Translators

———

Amphibious.

That's what I am.

And there are lots of us.

My friend the author Sandra Cisneros refers to herself as an amphibian because she lives in two different worlds and can serve as a bridge between Mexico and the United States. But at the age of fifty-seven, Sandra packed up her things, crossed the border—heading south—and settled back down in San Miguel de Allende, in the state of Guanajuato, Mexico. "I feel more at home, happier, and more connected to my community," she explained to me. "I feel very safe there. The neighbors are looking out for you. Back in the United States, I was afraid that I would die and my dogs would eat me, that nobody would find me until days later. That would be impossible in Mexico. Someone is always knocking on my door. *Gas? Water? Doñita?*"

The ideas of home and relocation have marked both Sandra's life and her books. She was born in Chicago and studied at the University of Iowa before going to teach in San Antonio. But in the United States, she told me, "I always felt like a foreigner." And ironically enough, this helped her become the writer she is today.

"I found my voice the moment I realized I was different," she wrote in her book *A House of My Own*. "I didn't want to sound like my classmates; I didn't want to keep imitating the writers I'd been reading. Their voices were right for them but not for me." This discovery gave birth to Esperanza, the protagonist of her famous novel *The House on Mango Street*.

In a lovely letter in which she paraphrased the poet David Whyte, Sandra wrote to me that "home is where you feel you belong." And so she went to live in Mexico.

I am also an amphibian, and I also feel like a foreigner in the United States. But unlike Sandra, I have decided to stay where I am. I think I've grown accustomed to the uncomfortable sense of being out of place, of feeling that there are those who don't want me here. And there are things that tie me to this nation—my children, my personal relationships, my job, and my work with other immigrants—that are much more important than the all-too-common shots taken by die-hard social media instigators.

"Amphibian" is the perfect word to describe my life in the United States. It comes from the Greek *amphi*, meaning "two" or "both," and *bios*, meaning "life." An amphibian is someone who inhabits two environments, combining two lives.

The word itself generally applies to either animals or military operations, but it comes in handy when talking about immigrants.

Being an immigrant means living in two places at the same time, sometimes interchangeably or even simultaneously. We come and go between the United States and Latin America, both literally and figuratively. There are times when Mexicans living in the United States spend entire days thinking about what's going on in Mexico, and at other times it doesn't even cross their minds.

Some people in Mexico refer to me as an American, whereas here I am considered Mexican. For those of us with dual passports, the border is simply a symbol. It doesn't really exist. We cross it heading north, we cross it heading south, and nobody stops us. We come from both sides of it.

It is a great privilege and a true honor to be part of a country. It's something I take quite seriously. But the fact is that I can instantly decide to be either Mexican or American. When I arrive at the Mexico City International Airport, I can choose the line that says "Foreigners" or the one for "Mexicans." And this decision doesn't require any deep philosophical analysis or carry any inherent feelings of guilt. In general, I travel with both of my passports, and I choose the line that's shorter. That's what determines which country I belong to at that particular moment. The official stamp on my passport shows what I chose to be on that day, but everything can change with my next visit.

It may seem strange that I can vote in two different countries, but for me it's a legal right that I worked hard to earn. I have the right to vote in the country that adopted me, the country where my children were born, where I have spent over half my life, and where I pay taxes. But I also have the right to vote in the country where I was born, where I grew up, where my family still resides and receives a portion of the remittances I send. Because of my profession and my personal interests, I pay very close attention to the political climate in both Mexico and the United States, and when elections are held, I know that the results will have very real consequences on my life and the lives of those around me.

I am now of two nations. That's the reality.

My accent—*chilango* in Spanish and Mexicanized in English—is like one of those leather suitcases that gets scratched by everything it touches, that changes over time and conforms itself to carry whatever is inside it. There are days when I can speak English with no major stumbling blocks, and there are others where I still sound like a newcomer. And no matter how much I study and practice, I will never feel as though I've mastered English to the degree that I've mastered Spanish. I sound exactly like what I am: a cluster of flowing currents and voices that collide, mix, and oppose one another.

It's impossible to be just one thing at a time.

I am many.

Immigrants understand that they are many things at once. We don't have a solid, immutable identity. Over the span of a single day, I can feel Latino, Mexican, American, foreigner, and newcomer. Other times the question doesn't even come up. The fact is that we don't wake up every morning and take a mental survey to identify what we are. This happens only when someone else brings it up or when we start scratching away at our own surface. Our sense of self is the product of multiple moving parts that operate within us and react with our surroundings. It is an unfinished portrait of who we are at one specific moment.

There are also days where I feel as if I don't belong to any country. I see the two governments, and they seem distant and unappreciative to me. But then something pulls me out of these abstractions and makes me part of a group, a home, a project on which we're working.

And since amphibians inhabit two worlds and handle two languages, we naturally evolve into translators.

It never ceases to amaze me when I hear stories about bilingual children who have to translate for their parents on the phone because their elders don't have a sufficient command of English. These children—temporarily converted into adults—bear a huge responsibility, often involuntarily. They are thrust into very delicate situations, whether they're talking about immigration, finances, taxes, or medical issues, and are thus transported into a foreign world. They are the youngest translators. To be a son or daughter is, at least in part, to be Mom and Dad's translator.

I come from this tradition.

It was never my job to translate English for my Spanish-speaking parents, but I spent the second half of my life translating it for others. Ever since the early 1980s, when I was starting out as a reporter for KMEX (Channel 34), the local Univision station in Los Angeles, I would go out and look for stories in any language I could find . . . but the report would have to be ready by six p.m. in Spanish.

I would speak Spanish almost daily with immigrants, but most of the local politicians preferred to communicate with me in English. Bringing information back and forth, leaping between one language and another, became quite normal, to the point where a simple greeting would let me know whether someone wanted to speak in Spanish or English. Now, the decision is almost instantaneous. Automatic, even. I say "hola" or "hello," and—depending on the language in which the other person responds, their accent, and their familiarity with the language of the initial greeting—the choice is made.

Some people—for instance, Eric Garcetti, mayor of Los Angeles, or Tim Kaine, U.S. senator and former vice-presidential candidate—immediately answer me in Spanish, even if they feel more at ease in English. Both of them do this to demonstrate their genuine interest in the Latino community. And there are post-Hispanic Hispanics such as Congressman Joaquín Castro, his brother Julián, former secretary of housing and urban development, and Senator Ted Cruz, who speak Spanish to some degree but always prefer to communicate in English. Some politicians will offer only a couple of words—*Hola, cómo estás*, or *Buenas tardes*—as if they were sending out a coded message to let me know they're Hispanic and that we have something in common.

During the first few moments of any interaction with a Latino, several decisions are made and many things are communicated nonverbally. Those of us who are amphibious and bilingual have to know what world we're coming from and which one we're entering. It's a quick and almost subconscious process. You have to adapt quickly to the situation presenting itself.

These days, contrary to my experiences early in my career, more politicians are learning Spanish so they can communicate more effectively with their Latino constituents. The examples I remember most are New York City mayors Bill de Blasio and Michael Bloomberg. Both took intensive classes to help them give interviews in Spanish. But most politicians don't do this; you have to interpret for them. What are they really saying?

Former president George W. Bush made a significant effort to communicate in Spanish during the 2000 election campaign that won him the White House. He had a great Hispanic adviser, Sonia Colín, who taught him a bit of Spanish and sensitized him to issues of great importance to the Latino community. I have jokingly referred to Bush as the first American president who thought he spoke Spanish.

But these steps are nothing to laugh at. It is entirely possible that many of the 537 votes that won him Florida (along with a little help from the Supreme Court) were from Hispanic voters, perhaps Cuban Americans, who heard his commercials and interviews in his rudimentary Spanish. Despite his struggles with grammar and pronunciation, Bush spoke to voters in their own language, making his intent clear.

Four years later, during the 2004 campaign, Bush used a similar communication campaign to win almost half—44 percent—of the Latino vote. It was thought then that, going forward, Republicans might have a real chance to split the Latino vote evenly with the Democrats. Bush wasn't willing to enact any immigration reform or suspend deportations, but his personal effort to communicate with Latino voters in Spanish—and his promise to treat Latin American immigrants "gently"—produced concrete results. His years in Texas served him well when he decided to go to Washington.

That was when some Latino voters could be wooed by a candidate who spoke a few words of Spanish here and there. But we quickly realized that it wasn't enough. Barack Obama borrowed the *Sí, se puede* cry of Cesar Chavez and Dolores Huerta. But Latino voters, disenchanted with Bush's empty words and invented wars, asked Obama for an explicit promise. What was he willing to give us in exchange for the Latino vote? His guarantee: An immigration reform bill would be on his desk, ready for his signature, during the first year of his presidency.

Ultimately, he failed to deliver.

And all of this has been translated.

Presidential candidates can reach Hispanic voters in many ways, but traditionally the most direct route has been through Univision, the television network where I've been working for more than three decades. After we made the first nationwide Spanish-language broadcast in 1981, back when the company was known as the Spanish International Network, President Ronald Reagan sent a message of congratulations and support.

Ever since then, any politician or candidate who wanted to communicate his or her message to Latinos in the United States would have to go through Univision, and it would have to be translated from English to Spanish. That was the route to take. Virtually every presidential candidate from the 1980s on has been interviewed on Univision, with the notable exceptions of Bob Dole, who lost, and Donald Trump, who won.

As a journalist, my job has been to translate these politicians who speak only English for an audience that prefers Spanish. In fact, the extraordinary interpreters with whom we work in Spanish prefer that term—"interpreter"—to "translator." And they're right. It is never a question of literal translations; rather, it requires interpretations of very complex subjects.

It is one thing to say that you support immigrants, but it's something quite different to say that you are in favor of legalizing undocumented immigrants or giving them a pathway to citizenship. There are politicians who support the Dreamers but are unwilling to offer legal support to their parents. And when a Mitt Romney or Donald Trump constantly refers to undocumented immigrants as "illegals," the interpreters must accurately reflect their words and prejudices.

While DACA and temporary protected status (TPS) cards guarantee residence in the United States for a limited period of time, and have been awarded to hundreds of thousands of Central Americans, they are not the same as green cards. The subtleties of the immigration debate are central to the lives of millions of people. An acronym can mean the difference between staying and leaving.

But according to most surveys, immigration is not the most important topic for Latino voters. The economy, education, jobs, and health care are also priorities. But immigration is the most emotional issue because it has the potential to end dreams and tear apart families.

This anxiety felt by millions of undocumented Latinos must be translated and communicated correctly. And it hasn't been easy. Many Americans, spurred on by Trump and his rank-and-file supporters, identify undocumented immigrants as criminals for simply having crossed the border illegally. They fail to understand that they are involved in a complicated economic phenomenon to which they are accomplices. Is this country willing to raise the prices on everything from hotels and restaurants to housing and food if massive sweeps of undocumented immigrants are conducted?

This is the correct translation of what's going on right now in the United States. As a journalist, my job is to translate what it means to be a Latino and an immigrant to the vast majority of Americans who do not speak Spanish. At the same time, on the nightly news, in my weekly columns, and every so often on social media, I have to communicate with Spanish speakers and report on the important issues happening in this country and around the world.

I translate from one part of the world to another. I report on Latin America for the United States, and vice versa, albeit in different ways. For me, Latin American affairs are like local news. It's common for me to know more about what's going on in Colombia, Venezuela, and Mexico than what's happening in Iowa, Kansas, or North Dakota, even though I am in fact closer to those parts of the United States. Yes, such a geographic disconnect does exist. I may be here physically, but emotionally and professionally I am crossing multiple borders.

In one way or another, we are all translators. Each of us has a very personal story to tell and comes from a universe that is often alien to others. As journalists, we have a responsibility to explain what we are seeing and hearing, particularly when we are traveling through remote locations and conflict zones. We translate symbols, conduct, and decisions to a distant audience.

When a reporter asks me what is the first thing he or she should do upon arriving in an unfamiliar place, my advice is usually this: Just tell me what you can see and hear, and leave the judgment for later. Take me to where you are. Be my eyes.

I am an immigrant with a microphone, and because of that, I am frequently invited to appear on CNN, Fox, and other networks in English to talk about the issues affecting other immigrants. I don't represent anything or anyone. But I do believe that part of my job is to give a voice to those who are not fortunate enough to be able to speak in front of a camera. It is all too easy to attack a group that has no political representation and cannot defend itself, such as the undocumented.

And when the government announces a new health care policy or changes existing immigration laws, my job is to read the fine print and explain what it means for the Latino community. My work as a journalist and translator is, ultimately, a public service.

Besides the headlines, my Spanish-speaking audience is looking for guidance and direction on issues ranging from health care and education to immigration and the voting process. And this is one of the fundamental differences with English-language news broadcasts. For many immigrants, the number one issue is how to survive in a new country with a different language that can often be hostile to your very presence.

That is why I consider journalism to be a public service.

And for that, you have to translate.

Amphibians are good at it.

When to Stop Being Neutral

———

Ajournalist's primary social function is to question those in power. Yes, you have to report the facts clearly and accurately. But once you have the data, you have to question—and in some cases challenge—the powerful.

This does not conflict with objectivity.

I agree with the principle of objectivity in journalism. As Professor Michael Bugeja of Iowa State University wrote in an article for the *Columbia Journalism Review*, "Objectivity is seeing the world as it is, not how you wish it were." I like this definition: it is clear, it shows intent to see things as they are, and it admits that reporters have prejudices and opinions and do not act in a vacuum.

There is, of course, no such thing as complete objectivity.

As soon as we decide to cover one story at the expense of another story in a different location, a number of subjective elements have already been introduced into the equation. Why do I cover the United States and not Nigeria or Vietnam? Still, though, once we decide to cover a story, the audience should expect journalists to display a reasonable level of objectivity. Our credibility depends on that. And if a journalist cannot be trusted, his or her work will have no value.

But being objective does not mean that we should always remain neutral. Sometimes neutrality runs counter to the truth itself.

Elie Wiesel's 1986 Nobel Peace Prize acceptance speech has had a profound influence on the way I view journalism. There are times when neutrality is not an option.

The world remained silent about the atrocities committed during the Holocaust, and that silence marked Wiesel for the rest of his life. As he said, "That is why I swore never to be silent whenever and wherever human beings endure suffering and humiliation. We must always take sides. Neutrality helps the oppressor, never the victim. Silence encourages the tormentor, never the tormented. Sometimes we must interfere. When human lives are endangered, when human dignity is in jeopardy, national borders and sensitivities become irrelevant. Wherever men or women are persecuted because of their race, religion, or political views, that place must—at that moment—become the center of the universe."

This applies to us all, not just to journalists. And, yes, sometimes we must intervene.

Even the most credible American journalist in history,

Walter Cronkite, did not believe in maintaining a blind sense of journalistic neutrality at all times. As he once said on NPR, "Early in 1943, I reported a bombing raid over Germany. In my lead, I wrote that I had just come back from an assignment in hell. But no one attacked our stories because they lacked objectivity. If neutrality is the test of integrity in journalism, then we failed in our duty to accord the Nazis fair and balanced coverage."

During that same program, Cronkite again touched on the subject in regard to the civil rights movement in the United States, saying, "Basic human decency was making editorial neutrality futile. Not since World War II had right and wrong seemed so clear cut. . . . But no amount of editorial neutrality could now rescue the South from itself."

What would Cronkite say today about the attitude journalists should assume with regard to Trump? That much is impossible to know. But from where I stand, suffice it to say that when you have a president who lies, who has made sexist, racist, and xenophobic comments, who attacks journalists and judges, and who generally behaves like a bully, you cannot remain neutral. He is the president, but that does not mean he is in the right. His behavior isn't a good example for adults in this country, let alone children. And if we remain neutral in spite of all this, we normalize his behavior and others will repeat it.

I'm passionate about the issue of journalistic neutrality during times of crisis, because journalists are the only ones who can challenge those in power with difficult and uncomfortable questions. At a 2017 TED Talk in Vancouver, I said the following:

I am a journalist, and I am an immigrant. These two conditions define me. I was born in Mexico, but I've spent more than half my life reporting in the United States, a country which was itself created by immigrants.

As a reporter and as an immigrant, I learned that neutrality, silence, and fear are not the best options, whether in journalism or in life. Neutrality is often an excuse for not taking action, for shirking our duty as journalists. And what is that duty? To question and challenge those in positions of power. That is journalism's true purpose. Its true marvel: questioning and challenging the powerful.

Of course, journalists are obligated to report reality as it is, not as how we would like it to be. And I agree with objectivity as a basic principle of journalism: if a house is blue, I'll say it's blue, and if there are a million unemployed people, I'll say there are a million.

But neutrality does not necessarily lead to the truth. While it is thoroughly balanced to present two points of view on any given issue—Democrat and Republican, liberal or conservative, government or opposition—this does not guarantee that I'm going to get to the truth.

Life is much more complex than that, and journalism must reflect that complexity. I refuse to be a simple tape recorder. That's not why I became a journalist. Of course, nobody uses tape recorders nowadays, so instead I'll say that I refuse to press "record" on a cell phone and face it forward like some fan at a concert.

That's not real journalism. Contrary to what many might think, reporters are constantly making judgments based on ethics, morals, and values, and they are always making decisions that are very personal and completely subjective.

What if you were a journalist in a country ruled by a dictator, like Augusto Pinochet's Chile or Fidel Castro's Cuba? Would you have reported everything the general and the comandante said without questioning them?

What happens when you learn that students are disappearing by the dozens, and that hidden graves are being unearthed? Or if millions of dollars suddenly disappear from the federal budget while a former president is becoming a multimillionaire? Do you only present the official version?

What if a presidential candidate for the world's top superpower were making racist, sexist, xenophobic comments? Well, that's exactly what happened to me.

In certain circumstances, journalists should not remain neutral. Not in cases of racism, discrimination, corruption, dictatorships, public lies, and violations of human rights. In these six cases, it is our obligation to set aside neutrality and indifference.

There is an extraordinary word in Spanish that perfectly describes the space that journalists should occupy. The word is contrapoder. *As journalists, our place is to always be standing opposite power.*

If you're in bed with a politician, if you attend the governor's son's wedding, or if you're simply a friend of the president, how will you be able to criticize them?

When I prepare for an interview with someone in a position of power, I think about two things. First, if I don't ask them an uncomfortable question, who will? And second, I operate under the assumption that I will never see this person again, and therefore I don't try to play nice or expect further access in the future.

If I have to choose between being a friend of the president or

his enemy, I would prefer to be his enemy. Being an accomplice
to power never makes for good journalism.

Putting aside our neutrality doesn't mean that we should
become partisan. Not with the Democrats, not with the
Republicans. Our strength and influence as journalists lie
precisely in our independence. And it is from that state of
independence that we must challenge power.

It's Just Television, That's All

———

There are times when I find it much easier to talk to a television camera than a person. It is, I admit, a professional defect. The late Morley Safer, mainstay of the program *60 Minutes*, once said with a hint of irony, "It is not natural to be talking to a piece of machinery. But the money is very good." Both statements are true.

Some of us who work in television sometimes forget that there are more important things in life. Much more important things. Television has dominated the public discourse for so many decades now that it can be hard for us to distance ourselves from it. When one is facing this problem, it can be helpful to remember a phrase often attributed to the comedian David Letterman: "It's only television."

Now is a good time to remember the fragile and ephemeral

nature of television. Executives are in denial when it comes to the digital revolution, just as newspapers and magazines have been for over a decade now. We find ourselves in a time of massive transition in which people's eyes are migrating from big screens to smaller ones. Plus, content consumption habits have become almost entirely personalized: people get the news when they want and where they want.

Every day I have to make multiple decisions that involve about three million pairs of eyes. Do I wait to report a story until the evening news is broadcast at six thirty, or do I break it through Twitter, Facebook, and other social networks? This dilemma is transforming the news industry. The money still lies in the commercials, which are linked to ratings, but the audience is leaving in leaps and bounds—or should we say clicks—for digital media. And ultimately, there is no fix: we must go where the audience is.

I'm a dinosaur. That's what I often tell journalism students. If you turn on the television one minute before or thirty-one minutes after the broadcast, you won't see me. That's the old way of watching TV. And if we don't adapt to the fluidity and ubiquity of digital media, we run the risk of going extinct. I'm fully aware of the fact that in this day and age I'm hosting a television show for many people who don't even have a TV anymore.

Things were very different when I started out as an anchor for *Noticiero Univision* on November 6, 1986. It's not that it was better or worse: it was simply the only one.

Spanish International Network was facing another internal crisis when the controversial Mexican journalist Jacobo Zabludovsky was set to become the head of the news agency.

Nearly all of the SIN reporters decided to resign en masse and start what would eventually become Telemundo.

I was working for a morning show, *Mundo Latino*, and since the channel was now lacking a male host, I was asked to present the news alongside Teresa Rodríguez. But I wasn't about to endure another bout of censorship. Before I accepted, I swore to myself that Zabludovsky would never reach the anchors' desk in Miami.

I was only twenty-eight years old, I had never interviewed a president, and I wasn't very good at reading the teleprompter. In complete solidarity, my friend Teresa would follow my script with her immaculate red nails in case I got lost while delivering the news. I will always be grateful to her.

It was clear to me that my status was a probationary one. For years, whenever I left to go on vacation, I would clean out my desk in case they found another anchor before I returned. It wasn't until I covered the fall of the Berlin Wall in 1989— three years after joining the newscast as anchor—that I learned my position would become permanent.

And it has been the greatest adventure of my life. A standard day might include a number of flights, presidents, interviews, and even a few battles on social media. When I spend the weekend at home, trying to rest and disconnect, it's because of the adrenaline rush I accumulate during the week. Being able to sit still and enjoy the silence is generally a good refuge. Some people go on vacation looking for extreme emotions or experiences. We reporters experience these things from time to time, but they come at a cost.

No matter how inured we, the communicators, become, I'm convinced that being exposed so often to violent imagery and tragic news takes a significant physical and emotional toll over time. Everyone who appears on television has learned to control their emotions in public. We aren't paid to break into uncontrolled laughter or tears on the air. But this affective suppression undoubtedly has negative effects on our personal lives.

The anchor of a newscast may appear to be in complete control. But few people understand all the little hints and tricks—and all the preparation—that it takes to master and control what is seen and what is said. It was always a treat for me to see Peter Jennings of ABC every time there was a breaking news story. He had a clear understanding of the subject matter and a seemingly effortless delivery. He could improvise as if he were talking with a lifelong friend. To be completely natural in the most artificial of mediums is a strange and unique talent, and Jennings had it.

But this is no longer the age of the anchor. I don't know how long this role will last. Not much longer, I expect, or at least not with the same leadership that Dan Rather, Barbara Walters, Tom Brokaw, Katie Couric, Ted Koppel, Connie Chung, Diane Sawyer, and my partner, María Elena Salinas, have had.

And that's another thing I tell journalism students: Don't look to become an anchor. Don't do what I've been doing for the past three decades. The idea of an anchor or broadcaster stems from the need to centralize the daily news, to deliver it through a single voice in a coherent and orderly manner.

Today, journalists should not be anchored. Don't become one. Do the opposite: become a journalist who can move from platform to platform, from country to country, who can skip effortlessly across borders, technologies, and languages.

But the fact that television journalism is undergoing such a dramatic transformation does not mean that journalism itself is at risk of going extinct. In fact, today it is more important than ever to have good reporters out there covering events. The only way to counteract so-called fake news is with more and better journalism.

There are two female journalists who have had a huge influence on my career: Elena Poniatowska of Mexico and Oriana Fallaci of Italy. In these two women, the words "journalist" and "rebel" are almost synonymous.

Whenever there is a doubt about what we, as reporters, should do when facing power, we should just ask ourselves, What would Elena do? And the answer is that she would continue to dig and report regardless of the consequences. Thanks to Elena and her book, *Massacre in Mexico*, we have invaluable firsthand testimony of the 1968 massacre in which dozens if not hundreds of students were killed by the Mexican Army.

Oriana Fallaci, the courageous Italian interviewer who confronted some of the most authoritarian leaders of the second half of the twentieth century, once said that being a journalist is both a privilege and a responsibility. I don't know any job that is more beautiful or more difficult. To us, nothing is foreign. The entire planet is our home. But we are also obliged to sing truths to the intolerant and to those in positions of power. And that can sometimes cost someone their life.

The killing of reporters is not new. What is new is the global influence and unquestionable independence of many journalists in the digital age. It represents the end of censorship. No government can make the Internet disappear. But having greater power and visibility means being a bigger target for intolerant groups and governments. This has been on display in Mexico.

According to the British human rights organization Article 19, more than a hundred journalists have been murdered in Mexico since 2000. Many of the killings have occurred in places where reporters are much more exposed to organized crime, drug traffickers, and corrupt politicians and police. Mexico is one of the most dangerous countries in the world to work as a reporter. These courageous journalists who refuse to remain silent despite threats of violence to them and their families, and who work far away from the nation's capital, are the true heroes of our profession.

I have often thought about what life would be like if I had stayed in Mexico. And still I do not know. Maybe I would still be feeling the same frustrations over the lack of freedom of expression that drove me to leave in 1983. But now it's no longer just about direct censorship by the government, but also about threats from criminal organizations operating with almost total impunity and with the tacit complicity of the government itself.

I don't know what I would be doing, but I do know that journalists are not in the business of keeping quiet.

Disobey!

———

A Letter to My Children

My dear Nicolás and Paola,

You happen to have an immigrant dad. What can we do? I know this has had an influence on both your lives and mine. But I think it's been good for us, hasn't it?

I know it's a cliché, but I have lived the American Dream to the fullest. I arrived here with very little, and now I have more. I left censorship behind me, and here I enjoy total freedom of the press. And most important, the two of you have many more opportunities than I ever did. I have nothing to complain about. We've received much more than I ever imagined. How could I not be eternally grateful to this country?

But despite all of this, I have to admit that some things still do scare me.

The fear of losing everything again. To be forced to start from scratch. Not being young enough to reinvent myself yet again. Sometimes I find myself doing what I did as a child in Mexico: saving what I have for the moment it becomes absolutely necessary, whether for an escape, an emergency, or anything else more important than the present. I have learned to live with very little—with what you might call a Japanese sense of simplicity—and I continue to worry about the uncertainty of what may happen tomorrow.

I don't believe in luck, or in saints or heaven. And it's hard to change this way of thinking when the formula has worked so well for so long. I have simply trained myself to be prepared for the exact moment when opportunity presents itself. And that's what I've done.

Now it's your turn. And you'll do it your way, not mine.

But as children of a very appreciative immigrant, I simply ask you to fight, to the extent that you can, so that other foreigners—those who came after me—will have the same opportunities that you and I have enjoyed. It's more than karma, more than a simple, ethical question: it's about giving back a little bit of what we've received. There is nothing sadder or more offensive than those who forget where they come from and who turn their backs on those who are trying to follow in their footsteps.

If you noticed, I used the word "fight."

It won't be easy. While demographic trends seem to confidently indicate that the United States is becoming a country comprised largely of minorities, there are many people who will continue to resist this change. Purity does not exist, and it is never a desirable goal for a nation to seek. Many massacres have taken place under the guise of this absurd ideal.

The great challenge facing this nation is whether we, as a people, can intelligently handle plurality in the face of the dangers of racism and intolerance. In a country where no single group will represent a majority of the population, it will become necessary to ensure that nobody can forcibly impose their beliefs on someone else.

But you're not alone.

The path has been clearly laid out by the Declaration of Independence, which affirms that all men (and women) are created equal. Our challenge is to continue to apply these principles to those coming from elsewhere, those fleeing persecution, those seeking a better future, and those who see and hear things differently . . . like your dad. The future of the experiment that is America depends on the results.

Let me say this to you: I have much more confidence in you and your generation than I do in the rulers who are currently looking to build walls and imprison immigrants. How quickly they seem to have forgotten that they, or their parents or grandparents, came from somewhere else.

Please, don't ever let that happen to you.

I recently found a wonderful quote to accompany us on this long and complicated journey. John F. Kennedy once wrote, "Immigration policy should be generous; it should be fair; it should be flexible. With such a policy we can turn to the world, and to our own past, with clean hands and a clear conscience."

In this paragraph we have all the indications for how we should treat immigrants in the United States: with generosity, regardless of their national origin or religion, and not only the wealthy and powerful but also the most vulnerable, and we must offer them the same rights that we ourselves enjoy. At this moment in our political history, it is known as immigration reform with a path to citizenship. And it's not a Democratic or Republican idea, but an American one.

That is the way.

I would like nothing better than to be able to tell you that everything will be all right, that a tolerant and multifaceted future awaits you, and that the racists of this world will never win. I hope that is the case. But what I can tell you is that things will be okay—or better—if you fight for them.

More than once, you've seen me fight on television with those who mistreat or criticize immigrants. Nothing is more unfair than attacking those who cannot defend themselves publicly. That is why I believe part of my job is to give a voice to the voiceless, and I'm afraid that often it will be up to you to do the same.

So here is my advice: Disobey.

When you are standing in front of a racist, disobey.

When they want to discriminate against you, disobey.

When they ask for something unjust, disobey.

When they can't publicly defend what they say in private, disobey.

When they demand loyalty above honesty, disobey.

When things have to change and there is no other way to do so, disobey.

Do it peacefully, but disobey nonetheless.

The American revolutionaries disobeyed the British. Rosa Parks disobeyed segregation laws in the South. Cesar Chavez disobeyed landowners in California. And the Dreamers disobeyed everyone, including their own parents, until President Obama granted them protection.

All the big changes—those that are worth fighting and risking lives for—begin when someone says "no." "No" is the most powerful word in any language.

That is the virtue of disobedience.

Use it carefully. Those who disobey don't always win, and they often pay a very high price for their audacity. But at least they have the peace of mind that comes with knowing that they did the right thing and, even better, that they were standing on the just side of history. The disobedient sleep better at night. The United States owes much to the disobedience of its immigrants, its rebels, its scientists, and its artists.

Together, Paola and Nicolás, we have been rediscovering this country.

You tied me to this land. In fact, I learned English and integrated myself into this country at the same time as you. I never could have imagined all of this when I first decided to launch this American adventure thirty-five years ago.

It reminds me of an interview I did with the Catalan Joan Manuel Serrat, one of my favorite singers whose lyrics—particularly "You make your way by walking" from the song "Cantares"—inspired me to journey north. Serrat, himself a tireless traveler, had to live in exile in Mexico during the Franco dictatorship in his native Spain.

As Serrat told me, "Not knowing how things will turn out can be a wonderful thing. I've always felt that no particular path was required. You can always leave one and pick up again on another; you can do different things, you can jump into another place. I've been able to travel as much as I've wanted, and I would love for the rest of mankind to have that same possibility, and to do so in freedom."

I have also been able to do most of my traveling in freedom. But, like Serrat, I do not know what the future holds. When I left Mexico, everything was uncertain. But today, I know that the two of you have, without a hint of doubt, been the best part of my life.

You know what, Nicolás and Paola? I could never have wished for better traveling companions on the road of life and country. It was all worth it for you . . . just for you.

I love you very much,
Dad

Acknowledgments

___

While most of what I'm writing here is new, I have also inevitably relied on speeches and interviews I have given and columns I have written in the past. Many of the ideas and arguments I present in these pages have appeared previously, in many different formats, on social media, in my weekly articles, or in my television commentaries. In some cases, I have left the original texts intact, when appropriate for clarity and consistency.

This book was made possible by all the immigrants—and the children and grandchildren of immigrants—who give me refuge. The bravery demonstrated by the Dreamers and their parents has been my inspiration. Each and every day I meet undocumented immigrants who fill me with hope. Their struggle is much more difficult than mine. I sincerely hope that some of your ideas, your proposals, and your courage are reflected in these pages.

In this book I have referenced a number of incidents that took place during the filming of the documentary *Hate Rising*. The director, Catherine Tambini, and producers Dax Tejera and Verónica Bautista were truly wonderful companions to have during the difficult and often disheartening trip across the country to document hatred in America on display. I would like nothing more than to work with them again on another project.

Isaac Lee's support for all the things that I do has been invaluable. He always says yes to my proposals, and I always have to double down and work twice as hard to meet his tremendous expectations. Daniel Coronell, president of news for Univision, is a great friend and office mate and the best guide through the difficult moments that journalism in the United States experiences. His years in Colombia were a true baptism of fire, and today they serve us all well. And Randy Falco, Univision's chief executive officer, has been an extraordinary moral leader when independent journalism and the Latino community need it the most. Randy, Isaac, and Daniel have always given me the support and freedom I needed to do my job well, and I know I can always count on them.

I also have to thank the multitude of researchers who provided me with the data and analysis with which to understand both immigrants and the growing Hispanic community. Much of the book is based on studies conducted by the Pew Research Center, the Migration Policy Institute, and the American Immigration Council and on Census Bureau statistics, among many other sources. Beyond the important surveys and data, I always give credit to the researchers. They are the ones leading the way.

Cristóbal Pera of Penguin Random House put all of his trust in this book before he had even read a single word. He is the one who wisely suggested that we give it the same title—*Stranger*—in both Spanish and English.

Ezra Fitz has translated so many of my books into English that sometimes I think I'm actually writing for him. Ezra is an amphibian extraordinaire. I write my books in Spanish, but his tremendous talent (and speed!) has allowed me to get to where I am in English. Ezra is the one who builds bridges.

Andrés Echavarría did all the necessary juggling so that I would have the time I needed—almost a year—to write this book. His enthusiasm for journalism and his incredible organization are the first things I see every morning when I get to the office.

Chiqui's passion for books, her unabashed feminism, her ever-present love, her practical advice, and her patience— granting me many months alone in front of the computer— made this latest delivery possible. Thank you again.

Several of the ideas appearing in these pages were first discussed with my daughter, Paola. It has been one of the greatest sources of pride and satisfaction that I have ever had, both as a writer and as a father.

Paola and Nicolás know that they are the two most important things in my life and that deep down everything I do is for them and because of them. The three of us learned to love this nation at the same time. If I want the United States to become even better, it is fundamentally for them and their generation.

Notes

————

PROLOGUE

5 **born to minority parents:** D'Vera Cohn, *It's Official: Minority Babies Are the Majority among the Nation's Infants, but Only Just* (Washington, D.C.: Pew Research Center, June 23, 2016), 23, http://www.pewresearch .org/fact-tank/2016/06/23/its-official-minority-babies -are-the-majority-among-the-nations-infants-but-only -just/.

GET OUT OF MY COUNTRY

10 **"When Mexico sends its people":** *Washington Post* staff, "Full Text: Donald Trump Announces a Presiden-

tial Bid," *Washington Post*, June 16, 2015, https://www
.washingtonpost.com/news/post-politics/wp/2015/06/
16/full-text-donald-trump-announces-a-presidential
-bid/?utm_term=.9d6229cd87a1.

13 "@Univision said they don't like Trump": *Hollywood Reporter* staff, "Donald Trump Bans Univision
Staff from His Properties, Publishes Anchor's Phone
Number," *Hollywood Reporter*, June 26, 2015, https://
www.hollywoodreporter.com/news/donald-trump-bans
-univision-staff-805464; Jordan Chariton, "Donald
Trump–Univision Battle Gets Nastier as Mogul Posts
Jorge Ramos' Cell Phone Number, Bans Staffers,"
Media Alley (blog), *The Wrap*, June 29, 2015, https://
www.thewrap.com/donald-trump-univision-battles
-gets-nastier-as-mogul-posts-jorge-ramos-cell-phone
-number-bans-staffers/.

15 come by plane or overstay their visas: Pew Hispanic
Center, *Modes of Entry for the Unauthorized Migrant Population* (Washington, D.C.: Pew Research Center, May 22,
2006), http://www.pewhispanic.org/2006/05/22/modes
-of-entry-for-the-unauthorized-migrant-population/.

18 my first exchange with Trump: "Donald Trump
Throws Fusion Anchor Jorge Ramos out of His Press
Conference," YouTube, August 25, 2015, https://www
.youtube.com/watch?v=AghbhqhHMgs.

22 my chance to confront Trump: "Jorge Ramos
Presses Donald Trump on Immigration at Iowa Press
Conference," YouTube, August 26, 2015, https://www
.youtube.com/watch?v=hD0PwbMdW7Y.

25 Romney earned only 27 percent of the Latino

vote: Mark Hugo Lopez and Paul Taylor, *Latino Voters in the 2012 Election* (Washington, D.C.: Pew Research Center, November 7, 2012), 4, http://assets.pewresearch.org/wp-content/uploads/sites/7/2012/11/2012_Latino_vote_exit_poll_analysis_final_11-09.pdf; see also http://www.pewhispanic.org/2012/11/07/latino-voters-in-the-2012-election/.

25 **31 percent of the Hispanic vote:** Mark Hugo Lopez, *The Hispanic Vote in the 2008 Election* (Washington, D.C.: Pew Research Center, November 7, 2008), i, http://assets.pewresearch.org/wp-content/uploads/sites/7/reports/98.pdf; see also http://www.pewhispanic.org/2008/11/05/the-hispanic-vote-in-the-2008-election/.

25 **27.3 million registered Latino voters:** Jens Manuel Krogstad, *Key Facts about the Latino Vote in 2016* (Washington, D.C.: Pew Research Center, October 14, 2016), http://www.pewresearch.org/fact-tank/2016/10/14/key-facts-about-the-latino-vote-in-2016/.

FAR FROM HOME

29 **Spanish author Javier Cercas:** Javier Cercas, *La verdad de Agamenón* (Barcelona: Tusquets Editores, 2006), 70.

30 **"the decision to migrate":** John F. Kennedy, *A Nation of Immigrants* (New York: Harper Perennial, 2008), 4.

STRANGER

36 **2010 Fortune 500 company founders:** Partnership for a New American Economy, *The "New Ameri-*

can" *Fortune 500* (New York: Partnership for a New American Economy, June 2011), 2, 6, http://research .newamericaneconomy.org/wp-content/uploads/2013/ 07/new-american-fortune-500-june-2011.pdf.

37 **"somebody else's babies"**: Mahita Gajanan, "Rep. Steve King Tweets Support for Far-Right Dutch Politician: 'Culture and Demographics Are Our Destiny,'" *Time*, March 12, 2017, http://time.com/4699168/steve -king-supports-dutch-politician/.

MY ROAD NORTH

45 **Mexican presidents were chosen *por dedazo***: Tim Weiner, "The Mexican Election: The Defeated; Political Machine Dependent on Power Loses Its Power," *New York Times,* July 4, 2000, http://www.nytimes.com/ 2000/07/04/world/mexican-election-defeated-political -machine-dependent-power-loses-its-power.html.

48 **rapid growth in the Hispanic population**: Antonio Flores, Gustavo López, and Jynnah Radford, *Facts on U.S. Latinos, 2015: Statistical Portrait of Hispanics in the United States*, Trend Data (Washington, D.C.: Pew Research Center, September 18, 2017), table 1-trend, "Population, by Race and Ethnicity: 1980–2015," http://www.pewhispanic.org/2017/09/18/facts-on-u-s -latinos-trend-data/.

THE REVOLUTION IS HERE

52 **non-Hispanic whites will cease to be the majority**: Sandra L. Colby and Jennifer M. Ortman, *Projections*

of the Size and Composition of the U.S. Population: 2014 to 2060, Current Population Reports, P25-1143 (Washington, D.C.: U.S. Census Bureau, March 2015), 1, 9, https://www.census.gov/content/dam/Census/library/publications/2015/demo/p25-1143.pdf.

53 **2044 projections:** William H. Frey, "New Projections Point to a Majority Minority Nation in 2044," *The Avenue* (blog), Brookings Institution, December 12, 2014, https://www.brookings.edu/blog/the-avenue/2014/12/12/new-projections-point-to-a-majority-minority-nation-in-2044/.

53 **non-Hispanic whites . . . Latino and Asian populations:** Colby and Ortman, *Projections of the Size and Composition of the U.S. Population: 2014 to 2060*, 9, table 2.

53 **Projections indicate that Hispanics will jump:** U.S. Census Bureau, *2014 National Population Projections Tables* (Washington, D.C.: U.S. Census Bureau, 2014), table 10, "Projections of the Population by Sex, Hispanic Origin, and Race for the United States: 2015 to 2060," https://www.census.gov/data/tables/2014/demo/popproj/2014-summary-tables.html; see in particular https://www2.census.gov/programs-surveys/popproj/tables/2014/2014-summary-tables/np2014-t10.xls.

54 **"the future is ours!":** 1984 Cesar Chavez Address to the Commonwealth Club of California, San Francisco, November 9, 1984, Cesar Chavez Foundation, Keene, California, http://chavezfoundation.org/_cms.php?mode=view&b_code=001008000000000&b_no=16&page=1&field=&key=&n=8.

54 **15 million Latinos to 14.9 million non-Hispanic**

whites: Phillip Reese and Stephen Magagnini, "Census: Hispanics Overtake Whites to Become California's Largest Ethnic Group," *Sacramento Bee*, June 30, 2015, http://www.sacbee.com/news/local/article25940218 .html; *Morning Edition*, "Census Data Confirms: Hispanics Outnumber Whites in California" (Washington, D.C.: National Public Radio, July 7, 2015), https:// www.npr.org/2015/07/07/420769494/census-data -confirms-hispanics-outnumber-whites-in-california.

54 **Latinos will represent 18 percent:** Vanessa Cárdenas and Sophia Kerby, "The State of Latinos in the United States: Although This Growing Population Has Experienced Marked Success, Barriers Remain," *Race and Ethnicity* (blog), Center for American Progress, August 2012, https://www.americanprogress.org/issues/race/ reports/2012/08/08/11984/the-state-of-latinos-in-the -united-states/.

55 **"Stories about Latinos" . . . 4.1 percent of the directors:** Frances Negrón-Muntaner, with Chelsea Abbas, Luis Figueroa, and Samuel Robson, *The Latino Media Gap: A Report on the State of Latinos in U.S. Media*, Center for the Study of Ethnicity and Race (New York: Columbia University, 2014), 3, https://fusiondotnet .files.wordpress.com/2015/02/latino_media_gap _report.pdf.

HATRED

58 **"a theory of 'activation' ":** Sanam Malik, "When Public Figures Normalize Hate," *Race and Ethnicity* (blog), Center for American Progress, March 25, 2016, https://

www.americanprogress.org/issues/race/news/2016/03/
25/134070/when-public-figures-normalize-hate/.

58 **hate groups in the country:** Southern Poverty Law
Center, Hate Map, 2016, https://www.splcenter.org/
hate-map.

58 **anti-Muslim groups . . . Ku Klux Klan:** Mark Potok,
The Year in Hate and Extremism, Southern Poverty Law
Center, Montgomery, Alabama, February 2017, https://
www.splcenter.org/fighting-hate/intelligence-report/
2017/year-hate-and-extremism.

59 **"The glorification of one race":** James Baldwin, *The
Fire Next Time* (New York: Dial Press, 1963), 82.

59 **"hate groups rail against non-white immigra-
tion":** Abraham H. Foxman, foreword to *A Nation of
Immigrants*, by John F. Kennedy (New York: Harper &
Row, 1964).

61 **"get the people that are criminal":** Julie Hirschfeld
Davis and Julia Preston, "What Donald Trump's Vow to
Deport up to 3 Million Immigrants Would Mean," *New
York Times*, November 14, 2016, https://www.nytimes
.com/2016/11/15/us/politics/donald-trump-deport
-immigrants.html?_r=1.

61 **three hundred thousand undocumented immigrants:** Muzaffar Chishti and Michelle Mittelstadt,
*Unauthorized Immigrants with Criminal Convictions:
Who Might Be a Priority for Removal?* (Washington,
D.C.: Migration Policy Institute, November 2016),
https://www.migrationpolicy.org/news/unauthorized
-immigrants-criminal-convictions-who-might-be
-priority-removal.

61 **11.2 million undocumented immigrants:** Sara

Kehaulani Goo, *Unauthorized Immigrants: Who They Are and What the Public Thinks* (Washington, D.C.: Pew Research Center, January 15, 2015), http://www.pewresearch.org/fact-tank/2015/01/15/immigration/.

62 **8.6 percent of adult U.S. citizens:** Sarah Shannon, Christopher Uggen, Melissa Thompson, Jason Schnittker, and Michael Massoglia, *Growth in the U.S. Ex-Felon and Ex-Prisoner Population, 1948 to 2010* (Princeton, NJ: Princeton University, 2011), 12, https://paa2011.princeton.edu/papers/111687.

62 **undocumented population . . . those who were born in the United States:** Walter Ewing, Daniel E. Martínez, and Rubén G. Rumbaut, *The Criminalization of Immigration in the United States* (Washington, D.C.: American Immigration Council, July 13, 2015), 1, https://www.americanimmigrationcouncil.org/sites/default/files/research/the_criminalization_of_immigration_in_the_united_states.pdf; see also https://www.americanimmigrationcouncil.org/research/criminalization-immigration-united-states.

63 **immigrants added $54.2 billion to the U.S. economy from 1994 to 2013:** National Academies of Sciences, Engineering, and Medicine, *The Economic and Fiscal Consequences of Immigration* (Washington, D.C.: National Academies Press, 2017), 171, https://download.nap.edu/cart/download.cgi?record_id=23550; see also https://doi.org/10.17226/23550.

64 **immigrants earn approximately $240 billion a year:** Laura Reston, "Immigrants Don't Drain Welfare. They Fund It," *New Republic*, September 3, 2015,

https://newrepublic.com/article/122714/immigrants
-dont-drain-welfare-they-fund-it; Jessica Lavariega
Monforti, "Immigration: Trends, Demographics, and
Patterns of Political Incorporation," in *Perspectives on
Race, Ethnicity, and Religion: Identity Politics in Amer-
ica*, ed. Valerie Martinez-Ebers and Dorraj Mano-
chehr (New York: Oxford University Press, 2009), 95,
https://www.researchgate.net/profile/Jessica_Lavariega
_Monforti/publication/269635089_Immigration
_Trends_Demographics_and_Patterns_of_Political
_Incorporation/links/5490e3170cf214269f27d5ab/
Immigration-Trends-Demographics-and-Patterns-of
-Political-Incorporation.pdf?origin=publication_detail.

THERE IS NO INVASION

66 **11.3 million undocumented immigrants in 2016:**
Pew Hispanic Center, *Unauthorized Immigrant Population
in the United States, 1990–2016* (Washington, D.C.: Pew
Research Center, May 3, 2017), http://www.pewhispanic
.org/chart/unauthorized-immigrant-population-in-the
-united-states-1990-2016/.

67 **Mexicans living in the United States . . . sixteen million Mexicans migrated:** Ana Gonzalez-Barrera, *More
Mexicans Leaving Than Coming to the U.S.* (Washington,
D.C.: Pew Research Center, November 19, 2015), 5, 7,
http://assets.pewresearch.org/wp-content/uploads/sites/
7/2015/11/2015-11-19_mexican-immigration_FINAL
.pdf; see also http://www.pewhispanic.org/2015/11/19/
more-mexicans-leaving-than-coming-to-the-u-s/.

68 **"principles of equality and human dignity":** John F. Kennedy, Letter to the President of the Senate and to the Speaker of the House on Revision of the Immigration Laws, July 23, 1963, American Presidency Project, http://www.presidency.ucsb.edu/ws/?pid=9355.

69 ***Wall Street Journal* report:** Neil Shah, "Immigrants to U.S. from China Top Those from Mexico," *Wall Street Journal*, May 3, 2015, https://www.wsj.com/articles/ immigrants-to-u-s-from-china-top-those-from-mexico -1430699284; see also Eric Jensen, "China Replaces Mexico as the Top Sending Country for Immigrants to the United States," *Research Matters* (blog), U.S. Census Bureau, May 1, 2015, https://census.gov/newsroom/ blogs/research-matters/2015/05/china-replaces-mexico -as-the-top-sending-country-for-immigrants-to-the -united-states.html.

A USELESS WALL

70 **Mexico and the United States share a border:** Sarah Trumble and Nathan Kasai, "The State of the Southern Border," *Third Way*, February 2, 2017, http://www .thirdway.org/memo/the-state-of-the-southern-border; Richard Misrach, "Surreal Photos Show Walls Dividing U.S. and Mexico," *National Geographic*, September 2017, https://www.nationalgeographic.com/magazine/ 2017/09/proof-border-wall-united-states-mexico/.

71 **"border communities" . . . "much safer than Washington D.C. or Chicago":** Julián Aguilar and Alexa Ura, "Border Communities Have Lower Crime

Rates," *Texas Tribune,* February 23, 2016, https://www
.texastribune.org/2016/02/23/border-communities
-have-lower-crime-rates/.

71 **"very safe, very secure area"**: Testimony of Sheriff
Tony Estrada to Congressman Raul Grijalva's Congres-
sional Ad-Hoc Hearing, Office of the Sheriff of Santa
Cruz County, Nogales, Arizona, September 13, 2013,
https://grijalva.house.gov/uploads/Sheriff%20Tony
%20Estrada.pdf; see also https://www.acluaz.org/en/
press-releases/arizona-congressman-us-mexico-border
-district-hear-regional-stakeholders.

72 **24.6 million Americans:** Substance Abuse and Mental
Health Services Administration, *Drug Facts*, National
Survey on Drug Use and Health (Bethesda, MD.:
National Institute on Drug Abuse, June 2015), https://
www.drugabuse.gov/publications/drugfacts/nationwide
-trends.

72 **a "scar":** Carlos Fuentes, *The Old Gringo* (New York:
Farrar, Straus and Giroux, 1985), 185.

73 **"that fucking wall":** Jorge Ramos, "Former Mexican
President to Donald Trump: 'I'm not Going to Pay for
That Fucking Wall,'" *America with Jorge Ramos*, February 25, 2015, https://fusion.net/story/273374/former
-mexican-president-to-donald-trump-not-paying-for
-that-fucking-wall/.

74 **between $12 billion and $15 billion:** Tom LoBianco,
Manu Raju, and Ted Barrett, "McConnell: Border Wall
Will Cost $12B–$15B," CNNPolitics, January 26,
2017, http://www.cnn.com/2017/01/26/politics/border
-wall-costs-republican-retreat/index.html.

74 **barely 150,000 immigrants:** Kennedy, *A Nation of Immigrants*, 17.

74 **a visionary study ... demographic tsunami:** Pew Research Center, *Modern Immigration Wave Brings 59 Million to U.S., Driving Population Growth and Change through 2065: Views of Immigration's Impact on U.S. Society Mixed* (Washington, D.C.: Pew Research Center, September 2015), 7–8, 10, 23, http://assets.pewresearch .org/wp-content/uploads/sites/7/2015/09/2015-09 -28_modern-immigration-wave_REPORT.pdf; see also http://www.pewhispanic.org/2015/09/28/modern -immigration-wave-brings-59-million-to-u-s-driving -population-growth-and-change-through-2065/.

NO ONE IS ILLEGAL

76 **"No human being is illegal":** Elie Wiesel, "The Refugee," in *Sanctuary: A Resource Guide for Understanding and Participating in the Central American Refugees' Struggle*, ed. Gary MacEoin (San Francisco: Harper & Row, 1985), 10.

77 **"the stigma of illegality":** Roberto Suro, *Strangers Among Us: Latino Lives in a Changing America* (New York: Vintage Books, 1998), 9.

80 **eight million could be subject to deportation:** Brian Bennett, "Not Just 'Bad Hombres': Trump Is Targeting Up to 8 Million People for Deportation," *Los Angeles Times*, February 4, 2017, http://www.latimes.com/ politics/la-na-pol-trump-deportations-20170204-story .html.

OBAMA: DEPORTER IN CHIEF

82 **Obama earned the title "deporter in chief":** Janet Murguía, "NCLR 2014 Capital Awards Speech: President's Message," *UnidosUSblog*, UnidosUS, March 4, 2014, http://blog.unidosus.org/2014/03/04/nclr-2014-capital-awards-speech-presidents-message/.

83 **2,749,706 people were deported:** U.S. Immigration and Customs Enforcement, *Fiscal Year 2016 ICE Enforcement and Removal Operations Report* (Washington, D.C.: U.S. Immigration and Customs Enforcement, 2017), 2, figure 1, https://www.ice.gov/sites/default/files/documents/Report/2016/removal-stats-2016.pdf; also see https://www.ice.gov/removal-statistics/2016.

84 **"an immigration bill that I strongly support":** Lukas Pleva, "No Big Push in First Year," *The Obameter* (blog), PolitiFact, August 13, 2010, http://www.politifact.com/truth-o-meter/promises/obameter/promise/525/introduce-comprehensive-immigration-bill-first-yea/.

85 **"what happened that first year?":** Fusion, "Why Didn't Obama Present Immigration Reform in His First Term? Rahm Emanuel Answers," Splinter, November 6, 2013, https://splinternews.com/why-didn-t-obama-present-immigration-reform-in-his-firs-1793840037.

85 **"Obama didn't move on immigration reform":** "Jorge Ramos Interviews Janet Napolitano (Nov. 2013)," https://www.youtube.com/watch?v=36p3FiUVMbQ.

86 **Deferred Action for Childhood Arrivals:** Jeffrey S. Passel and Mark Hugo Lopez, *Up to 1.7 Million Unauthorized Immigrant Youth May Benefit from New Deporta-*

tion Rules (Washington, D.C.: Pew Research Center, August 14, 2012), 3, http://assets.pewresearch.org/wp-content/uploads/sites/7/2012/12/unauthroized_immigrant_youth_update.pdf; see also http://www.pewhispanic.org/2012/08/14/up-to-1-7-million-unauthorized-immigrant-youth-may-benefit-from-new-deportation-rules/.

86 **"why did you deport two million people?":** "TRANSCRIPT: President Obama Speaks to Jorge Ramos," Fusion, December 9, 2014, https://wearefusion.tumblr.com/post/104812486184/transcript-president-obama-speaks-to-jorge-ramos.

88 **58 percent of all deportees:** *Fiscal Year 2016 ICE Enforcement and Removal Operations Report*, 2, 4, 11.

88 **300,000 had committed a felony:** Chishti and Mittelstadt, *Unauthorized Immigrants with Criminal Convictions.*

88 **Obama deported 409,849:** Corey Dade, "Obama Administration Deported Record 1.5 Million People," *It's All Politics* (Washington, D.C.: National Public Radio, December 24, 2012), https://www.npr.org/sections/itsallpolitics/2012/12/24/167970002/obama-administration-deported-record-1-5-million-people.

89 **240,000 in his final year of governance:** U.S. Immigration and Customs Enforcement, *Fiscal Year 2016 ICE Enforcement and Removal Operations Report*, 11.

90 **Obama won 67 and 71 percent of the Latino vote:** Cindy Y. Rodriguez, "Latino Vote Key to Obama's Reelection," CNNPolitics, November 9, 2012, http://www.cnn.com/2012/11/09/politics/latino-vote-key-election/index.html.

90 **Trump garnered only 29 percent:** Roberto Suro, "Here's What Happened with the Latino Vote," *New York Times*, November 9, 2016, https://www.nytimes .com/interactive/projects/cp/opinion/election-night -2016/heres-what-happened-with-the-latino-vote.

OUR 2016 MISTAKE

91 **27.3 million Latinos . . . Latino voters are millennials:** Jens Manuel Krogstad, Mark Hugo Lopez, Gustavo López, Jeffrey S. Passel, and Eileen Patten, *Millennials Make Up Almost Half of Latino Eligible Voters in 2016; Youth, Naturalizations Drive Number of Hispanic Eligible Voters to Record 27.3 Million* (Washington, D.C.: Pew Research Center, January 2016), 4, http://assets .pewresearch.org/wp-content/uploads/sites/7/2016/01/ PH_2016.01.19_Latino-Voters_FINAL.pdf; see also http://www.pewhispanic.org/2016/01/19/millennials -make-up-almost-half-of-latino-eligible-voters-in -2016/.

92 **only 47.6 percent . . . Many Latinos complain:** Jens Manuel Krogstad and Mark Hugo Lopez, *Black Voter Turnout Fell in 2016, Even as a Record Number of Americans Cast Ballots* (Washington, D.C.: Pew Research Center, May 12, 2017), http://www.pewresearch.org/fact-tank/ 2017/05/12/black-voter-turnout-fell-in-2016-even-as-a -record-number-of-americans-cast-ballots/.

93 **September 2015 *Washington Post*/ABC News poll:** *Washington Post*/ABC News poll, August 26–30, 2015, http://apps.washingtonpost.com/g/page/politics/

washington-post-abc-news-poll-august-26-30-2015/ 1811/; Aaron Blake, "Why Jeb Bush Could Be the GOP's Key to the Latino Vote," *Washington Post*, September 2, 2015, https://www.washingtonpost.com/ news/the-fix/wp/2015/09/02/in-bush-and-trump-the -gop-faces-two-opposite-paths-on-minority-outreach/ ?utm_term=.3c827ae4aafa.

93 **September 2016 *Wall Street Journal*/NBC News poll:** Carrie Dann, "Poll: 78 Percent of Latinos Have Negative View of Donald Trump, NBC News," September 22, 2016, https://www.nbcnews.com/politics/2016 -election/poll-78-percent-latinos-have-negative-view -donald-trump-n652311; Hart Research Associates/ Public Opinion Strategies, Study #16804, September 2016, https://www.scribd.com/document/324857651/ 16804-NBCWSJ-Telemundo-September-Hispanic -Oversample-Final.

93 **John McCain earned 31 percent in 2008:** Lopez, *The Hispanic Vote in the 2008 Election*, i.

93 **Mitt Romney's support dropped:** Lopez and Taylor, *Latino Voters in the 2012 Election*, 4.

93 **George W. Bush gained:** For the 2000 election: Roper Center for Public Opinion Research, *How Groups Voted in 2000* (Ithaca, NY: Cornell University, 2000), https:// ropercenter.cornell.edu/polls/us-elections/how-groups -voted/how-groups-voted-2000/. For the 2004 election: Roberto Suro, Richard Fry, and Jeffrey Passel, *Hispanics and the 2004 Election: Population, Electorate, and Voters* (Washington, D.C.: Pew Research Center, June 27, 2005), 12, http://assets.pewresearch.org/wp-content/

uploads/sites/7/reports/48.pdf; see also http://www
.pewhispanic.org/2005/06/27/iv-how-latinos-voted-in
-2004/.

93 **29 percent of Latinos:** Suro, "Here's What Happened
with the Latino Vote."

95 **3,640,000 Hispanics:** Mark Hugo Lopez, "The
November Election," *The 2016 Election and the Latino Vote*
(Washington, D.C.: Pew Research Center, 2016), 12,
http://www.ncsl.org/documents/taskforces/lopez_NCSL
_dec_2016.pdf.

96 **two-thirds of the Latino vote:** Leslie Sanchez, "Don't
Pigeonhole Hispanic Voters," CNN, October 8, 2010,
http://www.cnn.com/2010/OPINION/10/08/sanchez
.hispanic.voters/index.html; see also Mark Hugo Lopez,
*Latinos and the 2010 Elections: Strong Support for Democrats;
Weak Voter Motivation* (Washington, D.C.: Pew Research
Center), ii, 5, http://www.pewhispanic.org/files/reports/
127.pdf.

96 **Bush won more than 40 percent:** Sanchez, "Don't
Pigeonhole Hispanic Voters."

96 **"Latinos are Republican":** Ed O'Keefe, "Top Latino
Republican says, 'Farewell, My Grand Old Party,' " *Washington Post*, June 22, 2016, https://www.washingtonpost
.com/news/post-politics/wp/2016/06/22/top-latino
-republican-says-farewell-my-grand-old-party/?utm
_term=.3a7dab743e5c; Cathy Booth Thomas, "Lionel
Sosa," *Time*, August 22, 2005, http://content.time.com/
time/specials/packages/printout/0,29239,2008201
_2008200_2008222,00.html.

96 **Hispanics tend to be very conservative . . . reaching**

out to Latino voters: Paul Taylor, Mark Hugo Lopez, Jessica Martínez, and Gabriel Velasco, "Executive Summary," *When Labels Don't Fit: Hispanics and Their Views of Identity* (Washington, D.C.: Pew Research Center, April 4, 2012), http://www.pewhispanic.org/2012/04/04/when-labels-dont-fit-hispanics-and-their-views-of-identity/.

97 an "autopsy report": Republican National Committee, *Growth & Opportunity Project*, March 2013, 8, https://assets.documentcloud.org/documents/623664/republican-national-committees-growth-and.pdf.

FEAR AND DREAMERS

101 allow undocumented immigrants to remain: Sara Kehaulani Goo, *What Americans Want to Do about Illegal Immigration* (Washington, D.C.: Pew Research Center, August 24, 2015), http://www.pewresearch.org/fact-tank/2015/08/24/what-americans-want-to-do-about-illegal-immigration/; Mark Hensch, "Poll: Most Support Path to Legal Status for Illegal Immigrants," *The Hill*, March 17, 2017, http://thehill.com/homenews/news/324435-poll-most-say-citizenship-path-top-immigration-priority; Karlyn Bowman, "Reading the Polls: Welcome to America? What Americans Say About Immigration," *Forbes*, February 14, 2017, https://www.forbes.com/sites/bowmanmarsico/2017/02/14/reading-the-polls-welcome-to-america-what-americans-say-about-immigration/#1a84c0224e6f.

102 2015 was particularly violent ... Mexicans are

killed and nothing happens: Antonio Zambrano: https://www.nytimes.com/2016/08/23/us/pasco -washington-police-antonio-zambrano-montes.html? _r=0. Rubén García: http://www.cnn.com/2015/05/ 18/us/texas-police-shooting-immigrant-killed/index .html. Ernesto Canepa: http://losangeles.cbslocal.com/ 2015/03/05/deadly-police-shooting-in-santa-ana-draws -mexican-governments-attention/.

LATINOS: THE STRUGGLE
TO DEFINE OURSELVES

107 **9.6 million Latinos were born in the United States:** Antonio Flores, *Facts on U.S. Latinos, 2015: Statistical Portrait of Hispanics in the United States,* Key Charts (Washington, D.C.: Pew Research Center, September 18, 2017), http://www.pewhispanic.org/2017/ 09/18/facts-on-u-s-latinos/.

109 **35 percent of U.S. Hispanics:** Ana Gonzalez-Barrera and Mark Hugo Lopez, *A Demographic Portrait of Mexican-Origin Hispanics in the United States* (Washington, D.C.: Pew Research Center, May 1, 2013), http:// www.pewhispanic.org/2013/05/01/a-demographic -portrait-of-mexican-origin-hispanics-in-the-united -states/.

109 **three out of four Latinos still speak Spanish:** Jens Manuel Krogstad, *Rise in English Proficiency among U.S. Hispanics Is Driven by the Young* (Washington, D.C.: Pew Research Center, April 20, 2016), http://www .pewresearch.org/fact-tank/2016/04/20/rise-in-english

-proficiency-among-u-s-hispanics-is-driven-by-the
-young/.

110 **television in English:** Taylor, Lopez, Martínez, and
Velasco, "Language Use among Latinos," *When Labels
Don't Fit*, http://www.pewhispanic.org/2012/04/04/iv
-language-use-among-latinos/.

111 **get their news solely in English:** Mark Hugo Lopez
and Ana Gonzalez-Barrera, *A Growing Share of Latinos Get
Their News in English* (Washington, D.C.: Pew Research
Center, July 23, 2013), http://www.pewhispanic.org/
2013/07/23/a-growing-share-of-latinos-get-their-news
-in-english/.

111 **a fascinating study:** Taylor, Lopez, Martínez, and
Velasco, "Executive Summary," *When Labels Don't Fit*.

112 **"post-Hispanic Hispanics":** Zev Chafets, "The Post-
Hispanic Hispanic Politician," *New York Times Magazine*, May 6, 2010, http://www.nytimes.com/2010/05/
09/magazine/09Mayor-t.html.

112 **"Latinos are not on a straight track":** Suro, *Strangers
Among Us*, 70.

BEING AN IMMIGRANT
IN THE TRUMP ERA

117 **"somebody speaking in an accent":** Terry Gross,
"Trevor Noah Says He Grew Up 'in the Shadow of a
Giant' (His Mom)," *Fresh Air* (Washington, D.C.:
National Public Radio, November 22, 2016), https://
www.npr.org/templates/transcript/transcript.php
?storyId=503009220.

117 **"a cluster of flowing currents"**: Edward Said, *Out of Place* (New York: Vintage Books, 2000), 295.

121 **"They have to go"**: Alexandra Jaffe, "Donald Trump: Undocumented Immigrants 'Have to Go,' " *Meet the Press*, NBC News, August 16, 2015, https://www.nbcnews .com/meet-the-press/donald-trump-undocumented -immigrants-have-go-n410501.

121 **"get them out so fast that your head would spin"**: Sopan Deb, "Trump Would Take 2 Years to Deport Millions of Undocumented Immigrants," CBS News, September 11, 2015, https://www.cbsnews.com/ news/donald-trump-it-would-take-up-to-2-years-to -deport-millions-of-undocumented/.

ON AMPHIBIANS AND TRANSLATORS

153 **"the moment I realized I was different"**: Sandra Cisneros, *A House of My Own: Stories from My Life* (New York: Alfred A. Knopf, 2015), 125.

153 **Esperanza, the protagonist of her famous novel**: Sandra Cisneros, *The House on Mango Street* (Houston: Arte Público Press, 1984).

WHEN TO STOP BEING NEUTRAL

163 **"Objectivity is seeing the world as it is"**: Brent Cunningham, "Re-thinking Objectivity," *Columbia Journalism Review* 42, no. 2 (July–August 2003), 24, http:// archives.cjr.org/feature/rethinking_objectivity.php.

164 **Wiesel's 1986 Nobel Peace Prize acceptance speech**:

Elie Wiesel—Acceptance Speech, on the occasion of the award of the Nobel Peace Prize in Oslo, Norway, December 10, 1986, https://www.nobelprize.org/nobel _prizes/peace/laureates/1986/wiesel-acceptance_en .html.

165 **Walter Cronkite ... once said on NPR:** Walter Cronkite, "Civil Rights Era Almost Split CBS News Operation," *All Things Considered* (Washington, D.C.: National Public Radio, May 30, 2005), https://www .npr.org/templates/story/story.php?storyId=4672765.

165 **2017 TED Talk in Vancouver:** Jorge Ramos, "Why Journalists Have an Obligation to Challenge Power," TED2017, Vancouver, British Columbia, Canada, 2017, https://www.ted.com/talks/jorge_ramos_why_journalists _have_an_obligation_to_challenge_power/transcript ?language=en.

IT'S JUST TELEVISION, THAT'S ALL

169 **Morley Safer:** *"60 Minutes'* Morley Safer Retires after 46 Seasons," CBS News, May 11, 2016, https://www .cbsnews.com/news/60-minutes-morley-safer-retires -after-46-seasons/.

173 ***Massacre in Mexico*:** Elena Poniatowska, *Massacre in Mexico* (New York: Viking Press, 1975).

174 **murdered in Mexico:** Freedom House, *Freedom of the Press 2017—Mexico* (Washington, D.C.: Freedom House, November 1, 2017), http://www.refworld.org/ docid/59fc67d84.html.

ALSO BY

JORGE RAMOS

A COUNTRY FOR ALL
An Immigrant Manifesto

For decades, fixing the United States' broken immigration system has been one of the most urgent challenges facing our country, and time and time again, politicians have passed the buck. With anti-immigrant sentiment rising around the country and elections on the horizon, it's no surprise that immigration reform is on every candidate's agenda. While some candidates offer viable solutions, others perpetuate negative stereotypes and unpractical resolve. Jorge Ramos fearlessly questions political tactics and has undoubtedly become the voice of the Latino vote in the United States. It is now more important than ever to remember the role immigrants play in enriching our economy and culture, and to find a way to incorporate the millions of productive, law-abiding workers who have been drawn to the United States by the inexorable pull of freedom and economic opportunity. Ramos argues that we have a simple choice: to take a pragmatic approach that deals with the reality of immigration or to continue a cruel and capricious system that doesn't work, wastes billions of dollars, and stands in direct opposition to our national principles.
Current Affairs/Immigration

VINTAGE BOOKS
Available wherever books are sold.
www.vintagebooks.com